Praise for *Code Four: Surviving and Thriving in Public Safety*

What a wonderful book. Having served in both operational and administrative positions with a peer support program I found this book to be a must read for all first responders. Dr. Glenn has once again put forth a wonderful outline of how to stay mentally tough and healthy throughout a career by outlining the how and what we need to know to be healthy!! I would recommend this book to anyone from the front lines to management.

Todd Smith, Law Enforcement Manager,
Adjunct Professor of Criminal Justice

First responders and dispatchers are continuously placing themselves in situations that challenge their resiliency and coping skills. This book lays out the human response to stress. It illustrates how the persistent highs and lows of the job take their tolls in addition to the extreme situations that responders find themselves in. As I turned the pages of this book, I found myself having repetitive "ah-ha" moments. The saying "knowing is half the battle" becomes extremely relevant when reading this book. The reader will find themselves better understanding feelings, moods, and different responses they have had throughout the years. This book is a must read for both the new and experienced responder. These lessons will help us keep responders in the fight and ensure better durability, both on the job and in life. We are a team. We are here for those who need us, but we are also here for each other. These lessons will help us to maintain sustainable professions during challenging times and make us better responders for the future.

Matt Paul, Captain
Austin/Travis County EMS

She "Gets It." As someone who doesn't read books, Tania's book *First Responder Resilience* had me drawn in. I read it cover to cover in two sittings. *Code Four: Surviving and Thriving in Public Safety* is just as intriguing, builds on everything from that book and adds much more. Tania has a certain knack for explaining things that even a cop (or firefighter) can understand and relate to. This is another Must Read! *Code Four: Surviving and Thriving in Public Safety* is a great book for Clinicians, Peer Support Team Members, First Responders and their families. In layman's terms, it goes thru many of the phases of what first responders experience in their careers from day one in the academy to post retirement. Not only does Tania "Get It," she pays it forward.

Michael Weil,
Driver/Operator Baltimore County FD

Code Four:

Surviving and Thriving in Public Safety

By
Tania Glenn, PsyD, LCSW, CCTP

No part of this publication may be reproduced, stored in a retrieval system, or transmitted in any form or by any means, electronic, mechanical, photocopying, recording, or otherwise, without the written permission of the publisher.

Text Copyright © 2019 Tania Glenn
All rights reserved.

Published 2019 by
Progressive Rising Phoenix Press, LLC
www.progressiverisingphoenix.com

ISBN: 978-1-946329-95-0

Printed in the U.S.A.

Editor: Jody Amato

Front Cover Photograph:
"Code Four: Surviving and Thriving in Public Safety" (Tania Glenn and Peer Support Team Members) by Jill Hays, (www.jillhaysphotography.com). Used by permission of the photographer, © Copyright 2019 Jill Hays.

Author Back Cover Photograph:
"Tania Glenn" by Jill Hays, (www.jillhaysphotography.com). Used by permission of the photographer, © Copyright 2019 Jill Hays.

Book cover and interior design by William Speir
Visit: http://www.williamspeir.com

*To my Peer Support Teams—
Thank you for saving lives. I love you all.*

Table of Contents

Introduction i

The Story Behind #suckitptsd iii

Chapter One: This Work Changes Everyone 1

Chapter Two: Balance and Perspective 11

Chapter Three: Physical Health 20

Chapter Four: Mental Health 31

Chapter Five: Trauma 49

Chapter Six: Large-Scale Events and Disasters 77

Chapter Seven: Special Operations 91

Chapter Eight: Retirement 106

Chapter Nine: This Is Our War 113

Resource List for First Responders 119

About the Author 120

Introduction

I have the best job in the world. I help the helpers. I have the privilege of caring for the most caring, giving, toughest, bravest, most altruistic people on earth. I help them get through their darkest days and worst times. They trust me to lead them through adversity, help them pick up the pieces, and get them back to their normal lives. The question most asked of me is how I continue to treat PTSD in emergency services. The answer is because I have the best patient population there is.

In February 1993, I watched in horror as federal and Texas state law enforcement agencies attempted to raid the Branch Davidian compound in Mount Carmel Center Ranch in Axtell, Texas. The initial raid—followed by a fifty-one day standoff with a madman whose master plan was to slaughter his followers—took a massive toll on all those involved.

I was three months away from finishing my master's degree at the University of Texas in Austin. On the day of the raid, I knew my calling was to work with emergency services. I went to school the next day and informed my professor that I wanted to work with public safety and assist with high-velocity events. She proclaimed that I was "nuts for wanting to do this." Today, twenty-seven years later, I write this book because of a most amazing career—that of caring for the hearts and minds of police, fire, and EMS, and because the field of public safety has reached critical mass.

Today the field is encountering astronomical rates of post-traumatic stress, suicide, and alcoholism. I have spent my career preventing, intervening, and treating first responders, to strengthen their resilience and keep them on track. My goal has always been to help public safety personnel remain productive, effective, and happy people.

Much awareness of these shortcomings and issues exists, but not nearly enough resources and plans for care are in place. In my book *First Responder Resilience: Caring for Public Servants*, I address the elements of a good plan, intervention techniques, and options for care. In my book *Code Four: Surviving and Thriving in Public Safety*, I try to take this perspective to the individual level and to offer a "survival guide" for first responders in order to keep them fit. My goal is to help all first responders to not simply survive their careers, but to thrive.

Please note that while I typically treat first responders and veterans, I believe this book also applies to corrections, emergency room personnel, and flight attendants, who are all first responders in different venues.

The Story Behind #suckitptsd

Welcome to #suckitptsd Nation!

The **#suckitptsd** campaign was started during the Summer of 2015 when a patient who was conquering PTSD sent this hashtag to me via text on a day that was particularly monumental in their recovery. **#suckitptsd** became a mantra, a motto and a campaign that resulted in an overwhelming response from followers on Facebook and Twitter.

Soon after, the same patient created the prototype for the wrist band that is now bringing together a community of first responders, veterans and active duty military members who want to raise awareness, fight PTSD, encourage resilience and help others. Over 17,000 wristbands have been distributed to first responders and veterans across America, and in Canada, New Zealand and Australia.

The wristbands are black and teal, as teal is the PTSD awareness color.

One of the best stories from the **#suckitptsd** history occurred between a veteran and a police officer in Arizona. The veteran had recently received treatment for his PTSD and was at a Veteran's Day parade when he spotted a law enforcement officer with a wristband. He approached the officer and held up his arm with his own wristband and he asked the police officer about his band. The two shared stories and encouraged each other to stay in the fight. This simple interaction represents a true culture change, the connection so many people share and the importance of healing together.

Chapter One

This Work Changes Everyone

*'Cause who I am
Isn't who I used to be
And I'm not invincible
I'm not indestructible
I'm only human
Can't you see
The beauty in me*

"Monster You Made" by Pop Evil

Public safety professionals enter their careers with passion and purpose. In almost 100 percent of interviews, first responders mention helping people as their primary reason for entering the field. The desire to right the wrongs, bring about justice, stop pain, intervene in crises, and save lives will drive amazing men and women to go to school and dedicate their lives to helping others. The calling is noble. It speaks volumes about the people who step up to do the mind-boggling, heart-rending work first responders do.

First responders who work in this field for their

entire careers or for prolonged periods of time generally go through three very distinct phases in their careers. I refer to the initial phase as "The Innocence." This first phase is marked by initial energy, excitement, and many difficult lessons learned. As first responders emerge from The Innocence phase, they move into phase two—"The End of the Innocence." This second phase happens when first responders have developed a very clear sense of reality, a sense of what their careers are all about. The End of the Innocence is when they struggle with burnout from the trauma they have sustained, the impact of their careers on their lives, and the decision of whether or not to continue this difficult job. If our public safety professionals continue on their career path, they enter phase three, which I refer to as "Wisdom." As first responders reach wisdom, they have chosen to continue their careers and head toward the finish line. They have learned to maintain a steady pace, can fly under the radar, stay out of trouble, and just get the job done. Now they just want to head toward the end of their careers with the goal of making it to retirement successfully. Many also include in their plans the desire to move away from the city where they live, and to end up on a ranch in the middle of nowhere so they never have to deal with people again.

The Innocence

As police officers, firefighters, EMS, and dispatchers begin their careers, they are full of excitement and energy. No one leaves school or training thinking they are going to save the world, but there is a mission and a purpose to help as many people as possible. New first responders are armed with skills and training that will be refined and improved upon in the first few years of their careers, along with an understanding of their role in people's lives, which will also change over time. Despite the fact that they understand they can't save the world, novice public safety personnel begin their careers with a sense of innocence and extremely high expectations. They set out with passion and purpose. They are full of compassion and the desire to assist, and they believe that they can and will make a difference.

Brand-new first responders love their jobs and frequently the job defines them. They eat, breathe, and sleep police, fire, and EMS. They buy new vehicles that reflect their career choices. They constantly work, sign up for overtime and extra assignments, and volunteer for extra duties and projects. Socially, first responders typically begin to alienate their "normal' friends – those eight-to-five people who no longer understand the first responder and who are perhaps confused by their vocabulary and sense of humor. They feel that it is much easier to hang out with like-minded people who understand what they are all about.

While this is an exciting time in a person's life and career, it is the beginning of the lack of balance that is so pervasive in the challenges that public safety personnel face. Work and work-related activities permeate the lives

Code Four: Surviving and Thriving in Public Safety

of first responders, and eventually they realize that their lives are out of balance. Work has taken over—family, faith, friends, hobbies, and any semblance of a life outside the job are gone.

In the first five years of their careers, first responders are handed a nasty dose of reality that can't be replicated in school. They meet people on the worst days of their lives. No one calls 911 because it's a good day and things are fine. Public safety personnel enter situations full of pain, illness, trauma, and horror. They encounter individuals who called 911 and who subsequently turn and attack them when they show up. They see death, destruction, accidents, violence, abuse, and they see evil. They are exposed to despair, poverty, and mental illness. On twenty-four and forty-eight hour shifts, they are awakened at two o'clock in the morning to blasting tones and flashing lights, with instructions to get up, get dressed, get out the door, and go to the person who is calling about toe pain. Meanwhile, this toe pain has reportedly been in existence for approximately two weeks, and no one thus dispatched may show an ounce of frustration. Public safety personnel are somehow expected to be immune or void of any normal human reactions in frustrating circumstances.

The simultaneous wake-up call for new first responders involves politics. New employees quickly begin to learn that there is a mind-boggling amount of policies and procedures, as well as consequences for every deviation from these policies. They learn about an enormous bureaucracy and an incredible amount of documentation that every department must complete in an effort to cover every legal loophole possible. Hours upon hours of documentation, report writing, and charting are spent during every shift, with a constant pressure to hurry up and get it done because calls are holding. Never mind that at the moment of immeasurable documentation and calls holding, a first responder is also physically dehydrated, fatigued, and has had no food in about eight hours. This same first responder might have started their shift with a write-up for violating a policy during the previous shift, which is a remarkably effective way to take the wind out of someone's sails. And yet the public expects them to deliver service with a smile—no exceptions.

The End of the Innocence

After a few years of working in public safety, most first responders have reached the End of the Innocence. They become hardened and callous. They sometimes begin to resent the public and typically view anyone outside of public safety as "assholes" or "idiots." At around five to eight years into this career, public safety personnel have lost the innocence, and they begin to view their jobs as cleaning up other people's messes. Rarely now do they connect to a victim, a patient, or a family member in a meaningful way. The underlying resentment is seen in hardened expressions and their attitudes.

Code Four: Surviving and Thriving in Public Safety

I frequently explain to public safety personnel that burnout is usually present between the five- and eight-year mark in their careers. It is hard to identify the onset of burnout because the course of burnout is akin to a slow simmer that eventually boils. First responders know that something is different, but it's hard to figure out exactly what is going on as they progress from the early stages of burnout to being completely on fire.

At this point they have options. They are facing a crossroads, and choosing which path to take is a very important decision. First responders can stay on the same path, and things will continue the way they are or even get worse. Another option is that they can quit altogether. The third option is the most challenging yet rewarding path. This option requires first responders to take a deep breath, take a step back, address their stressors and traumas, engage in self-care, and regain balance. This is the work we do now in cadet, annual, and recurrent training and in therapy. It is never too late to regain balance, but realizing it sooner rather than later certainly lends itself to a quicker recovery.

Early in my career I had a patient with remarkable burnout: HE WAS DONE. He hated his job, his life, his patients, his colleagues—you name it. Everything and everyone were on his shit list. Jeff was a paramedic in a very busy system. He struggled with finding the motivation to get to work each shift and to drag himself through each twenty-four hours. Jeff's burnout extended into his personal life. His wife was done with the marriage.

Jeff's kids were afraid of him to the point that when he walked into the same room where they were, the kids would immediately stop talking. One day when he was expressing how his children behaved around him, I half-jokingly referred to Jeff as a "family terrorist." He looked at me and indicated that this was, in fact, very true. Jeff asked me to help him change.

During one session, Jeff was expressing how numb he felt all the time. I asked him to tell me about the last time he felt something. At this point Jeff looked up, paused, and looked back at me. "Three years ago, on a call." Not exactly what I expected to hear. Internally my response was "Wow!" Externally, however, with my therapist poker face, I asked Jeff to tell me about the call. Jeff indicated that it was an infant SIDS death. When they called for the pronouncement, the mother began to wail. As she shrieked and cried, Jeff told me he began to tear up and developed a lump in his throat. His youngest was the same age as the infant he had just pronounced dead. Jeff did what he had to do at the time—he sucked it up, he shut down his emotions, and he drove on. What he failed to do in the aftermath, however, caused the problem. He forgot to process the call. He forgot to ask for help. And he forgot to reset himself back to being a father and husband.

I challenged Jeff to regain the balance and perspective in his life, which is the focus of Chapter Two. Jeff took it on. He trusted me and jumped in with both feet. Jeff continues to this day as a public servant with a life outside the job, because he realized he needed to change and he asked for help.

Wisdom

Wisdom causes gray hair. It involves hard lessons learned and a few scars along the way. As first responders continue their careers with the goals of retiring and enjoying their retirement, they reach the third stage in their careers: Wisdom. Public safety personnel learn to maintain a steady tempo. They learn to manage their frustrations by not taking situations personally. Instead of referring to the public as "assholes and idiots," they refer to them as "job security." Public safety personnel who are in this final phase understand the big picture and have confidence in their skills and their abilities to handle difficult situations well. Sometimes they are promoted, sometimes they stay on the line. Whatever they choose, first responders in this third phase are battle-torn and tired, but they have an internal resolve to keep going and make the most of it while they can.

One thing I have noticed about first responders in the third phase of their careers is that many of them are compassionate and patient. Many public safety professionals late in their careers have come to see me about this strange new "thing" going on inside of them. They explain how difficult it is when they are getting a pronouncement for a time of death and subsequently delivering a death notification. One firefighter told me that during a death notification, he began to tear up and got a lump in his throat. He asked me what this was. I told him this was "the f word." He looked at me curiously and I explained he was having *feelings*. He looked right at me and told me, "No, not that! Not those. I don't do those."

By the time first responders have reached phase three, they have also lived life. They have lost people they love. They truly understand the innocence and helplessness of vulnerable populations. They typically have older or grown kids and even grandchildren. The wisdom that comes with life is hard-earned and causes a lot of gray hair. What I tell first responders is that their compassion, care, and the wisdom they bring to a crisis is invaluable. I explain that the family members receiving the death notification will never forget the kindness, concern, and genuine connection these amazing frontline folks offer them. I also validate the fact that this is very draining and that self-care after a tough call is extremely important. The bottom line is: when someone is in crisis and their world is turned upside down, the skills and personal connection first responders bring to the situation are the most valuable part of that person's recovery.

Special Considerations for Loved Ones

Today's public safety career can be a bumpy ride for family members who experience the changes in their loved ones but frequently do not know how to respond to them. No one should downplay the impact on family members and friends. Loved ones who are not in the field of public safety are subjected to personality changes in their first responder, massive vocabulary and terminology changes, shift work, critical incidents, burnout, department politics, and trauma.

Proactive departments train loved ones on what to expect. Unfortunately, this important phase is often neglected. Departments that value their employees understand that they must also extend care and contact to families. They must offer resources, support, and guidance. They must hold "family days" and encourage family members to "ride along."

The main advice I give family members is to get educated, ask for help when they need it, and try not to get overwhelmed. I advise first responders and their families to slow down, take time to communicate, and to engage in relationship counseling when they need it. Every relationship needs an occasional tune-up. The key for first responders is to understand that just because they fix other people's problems rapidly for a living, it does not apply to their own relationship. If a first responder family enters a crisis, then by all means, get into mission mode. But when it comes to communication, raising kids, balancing work and home life, or managing a budget, dealing with in-laws, and the existence of hurt feelings and repeated arguments couples have, they must understand that their role as law enforcement, fire, and EMS does not apply. Home life is not a 911 call.

Chapter Two
Balance and Perspective

*I'm fade to black as a search for the light
Can you bring me back from this unconscious life?
Can you show me the way I'm lost in the dark
I've fallen apart, can you unbreak my heart?*

"Breathe" by Through Fire

A few years ago, a flight paramedic from another state was sent to me by his company. While he was senior in rank and time served, he had not been able to mentally climb his way to the Wisdom phase. Despite his many years on the job, he was very much still in the End of the Innocence phase and extremely burned out.

The event that prompted Mark's employer to send him to me was the day he pulled into the parking lot of his base, called his supervisor from his vehicle, and explained his situation: He was in total despair. He could not take another call, he could not get on another flight, he could not treat another patient. Mark was done.

Mark is still a flight paramedic, and he loves his job. Not surprisingly, his passion is helping other flight crews in preventing burnout and keeping balance in their lives.

While Mark and I certainly dealt with the trauma resulting from career occurrences, including tough patients from scene flights and inter-agency transfers, the majority of the work we had to do was to restore balance in his life and address his perspectives.

Balance

Achieving balance is one of the most important ways to build resilience. Having a good sense of balance with career, family, and personal time is essential to well-being. For first responders, achieving balance can be challenging.

When I speak to young public safety personnel who are just entering the field, I always make several points on maintaining balance. In the early phase of someone's career, it is all preventable, which is a luxury. Addressing these points with the more seasoned first responders, when balance has gone awry, means that some important aspect of their lives needs changing. This is more challenging. Here are two factors to maintain balance:

Keep the friends you have now or reconnect with your old friends.

When first responders enter the field, they are met with many challenges to balancing their work schedules and work lives with the rest of the world. Since first responders work everything but an eight-to-five schedule, their time off does not jive with what I refer to as "the normal people." Days off are different, and draining shift work does not make connecting with others on days off easy. Rotating days off also prohibits spending time with normal eight-to-five friends. Over time, the challenges associated with spending time with friends outside of work eventually decreases the motivation of first responders to spend time with normal friends. Consequently, over time, public safety personnel choose to hang out with their own colleagues, rather than their non-public safety friends.

Another component of isolating from normal friends is the fact that these friendships tend to grow apart because of the difference in life experiences. First responders frequently tell me that their friends from their former lives do not understand them anymore. These normal friends question what they do, don't understand the aspects of the job, comment on their personality changes, and question their sense of humor. First responders eventually give up on their old friends. They chalk it up to the fact that they "just don't get it."

As tempting as it is to hang out with like-minded colleagues who share the same experiences, perspective, vocabulary, and beautifully twisted sense of humor, when first responders only spend time with colleagues, they mentally never get away from work. An evening spent sharing stories about calls, talking about rumors at work, addressing department politics, and griping about the bullshit at the job keeps first responders mentally at work. While I think it is important to spend time with colleagues and have evenings like this, it is also just as important to spend time with your normal friends and have different types of interactions.

The key to spending time with those normal friends is to consciously make an effort to talk about life outside of public safety work. There are a million things to talk about in this world besides cool calls, bad calls, kid calls, shitty calls, and bullshit calls. Ask those normal friends not to ask you about work, or the worst thing you have ever seen, or if you have shot someone. Have conversations about anything else. The more first responders challenge themselves to get outside of their public safety world mentally, the more they realize it's a nice break to spend time with others where their work does not come up.

Have a life outside the job.

Families, hobbies, interests, and joy—these are the traits I see in the most resilient first responders. Given the demands on public safety personnel, these are also the factors that are easily put on the back burner. Resilient first responders dedicate time and energy to prioritizing their important aspects of life.

In my practice, an air medical customer had an incident involving an incapacitated pilot that significantly traumatized the flight crew. Based on the trauma, my assumption was that they were going to need quite a bit of care. I could not have been more wrong.

When the crew members came to see me, they certainly were not okay with the incident. However, they were motivated to overcome the event. The work we did involved evidence-based trauma interventions, including Eye Movement Desensitization and Reprocessing. Both bounced back from the incident with ease. I could merely claim 5 percent of credit for their recovery, for the amazing paramedic and nurse both had significantly high degrees of resilience. They love their jobs, love flying, and love their patients. They have hobbies. They hunt, fish, hike, swim, and play sports. They have amazing families. They both tackle personal issues when presented with challenges. They both use alcohol only in moderation. They are both truly amazing people, clinicians, and patriots. All of this is the other 95 percent of the reason they healed so quickly.

The most important thing to realize about balance is that because emergency services is a culture and a lifestyle, first responders must give themselves permission to have a life outside the job. Yes, it is okay to enjoy your time off, forget about work, have fun, and take time to be mentally and physically away from the job. The longer someone has been doing this job, the more challenging the achievement of balance will be. The bottom line is this: if you are good to yourself, you are even better to your colleagues and to the public.

Perspective

As I was growing my private practice, I worked full-time in a Level II trauma emergency room. My usual shift was Friday, Saturday, and Sunday nights. I spent three nights a week, twelve hours each night, in the midst of chaos and suffering. I remember many mornings as I was clocking out, I would brace myself as I opened the door to the outside world, fully expecting to see the same madness I had just experienced all night long. I was ready to duck for cover to avoid shootings, stabbings, getting hit by drunk drivers, and whatever else had come our way that night.

Instead, as I walked toward the parking garage, I would see runners training for their next race, families with babies in strollers enjoying the morning, birds chirping in the trees. I would wonder where all the chaos was, until I realized that my perspective was completely skewed. While we had a steady flow of craziness in the emergency room, the madness was condensed in one place. The vast majority of the rest of the city was just fine.

First responders, by nature of their role, walk into the worst days of people's lives. No one calls 911 because things are going well. Emergency services crews respond to stop violence, pain, suffering, death, and destruction. They see people at their worst on the worst days of their lives. They are lied to frequently in order to cover up crime or bad behavior, and they are often left sorting out fact from deceit in a very short amount of time.

Ironically, the chaos and violence is counterbalanced by calls for complaints such as toe pain, typically at two o'clock in the morning. Public safety personnel also deal with the destitute, who frequently have no option but to call 911 to help them manage their lives.

It is very easy to forget over time that the function of emergency services is to manage and take control of any situation, no matter how abnormal. Public safety professionals are exposed so frequently to the abnormal, they often begin to consider what they see as the norm. When this happens, first responders struggle with how they see the world, the public, and how they see humanity and people in general.

I always remind public safety professionals that every time they are driving code three toward a situation, they are passing hundreds, if not thousands, of happy, healthy people who do not need them. These are the people who are leading good lives and having normal days. They appreciate first responders for who they are and what they do, but they rarely, if ever, need you. If and when they do, they will call. By the nature of the job, first responders do not interact with normal, happy, healthy people because their paths do not cross.

Unfortunately, what this does for many first responders is it creates a distance between them and the population that is grateful for them. The happy, healthy people are lumped into the same category as the people who spit on and attack first responders. There is never a chance to really meet and connect with the happy and healthy category.

I frequently ask emergency service professionals to take a look around when they are in public. I ask them to really see the protective parents, the happy children, and the kind acts strangers do for each other. I also make it a point to remind them how much the public loves law enforcement, fire, and EMS. When a first responder is in need, the general public loves to help. When a first responder is killed, they line streets to wave flags and show respect. Don't forget about these people. They are all around you, and they love you because of who you are and what you do.

Special Considerations for Loved Ones

While it can be uncomfortable and challenging to see your loved one transition from the person you have known to someone who is hardened and jaded, it is important to understand that this is normal. It is not a reflection of your loved one's personality; it is a coping mechanism all first responders use to cope with the negativity and stress of the job.

I always encourage an open dialogue and acknowledgement of changes first responders go through, as well as ways to keep it all in check. In other words, have a discussion on ways to minimize the negative impact your work might be having on you and your family. Encourage your first responder to remember that the wall they build for the outside world does not have to be up when they walk through the front door or that it is okay to let that wall down slowly if necessary.

Finally, the most successful couples are the ones that figure out their relationship modus operandi in terms of managing their personal lives and their public safety careers. Deciding on how much time you want to spend talking about work versus the rest of life, understanding that your first responder might need space and time to decompress from a shift, being there to listen without judging (which goes both ways), and embracing the fact that this career is not like any other are all ways to mitigate the impact of the job on home life.

Chapter Three
Physical Health

Get up, get up
Get a move on
Get up, get up
What's taking so long
Get up, get up
Get a move on
Stop stalling, I'm calling out

"Get Up" by Shinedown

First responders spend their careers helping others. Whether protecting a person's legal rights, mitigating imminent health threats, rescuing people when an accident occurs or when disaster strikes, or simply consoling someone on a bad day, first responders are always ready to take the call and rise to the occasion. What amazes and saddens me, however, is how little first responders care for themselves. Over time, many public safety professionals fall into the trap of giving everything of themselves to others, while giving nothing to themselves.

Physical health is one of the most important aspects of public safety. It is hammered home in every academy and demonstrated by instructors to create a mindset that health and fitness are a priority. Many first responders let their health go because they believe they don't have the time, energy, or desire to care for themselves. Given the amount of weight a first responder carries in equipment and body armor, being suddenly confronted by someone under the influence of drugs with super-human strength can be a real danger to the health of first responders.

Exercise

One of the most important contributors to both physical and mental health is exercise. The worst thing you can do for your physical and mental health is to quit working out. And yet, one of the first things public safety personnel give up when they are struggling is exercise.

Working out has a plethora of benefits for your health, including stress management and lower cholesterol. Exercise enhances concentration, improves mood, and combats depression. People who work out stay sharp mentally and have less tension and anxiety. They also sleep better.

The first key to exercise is to just move your body. If running hurts your knees, don't run. Do what makes you feel good. You don't need to push yourself until you are sore. This will only discourage you. Just start moving your body.

The second key to exercise is to ease into it. When my patients begin to work out again, I discourage anything that will set them up for failure. I don't necessarily want them to join a gym, pay lots of money, and go a few times only to get discouraged, sore, and frustrated.

I had a former patient who told me that he likes to walk his dog. I asked him to walk his dog twice in the first week as goal number one, which he did. He was very encouraged to take on a totally feasible and fun fitness assignment. For week two, I asked him to walk his dog three times. On week three, he walked his dog four times, which was his assignment, and he dusted off the rowing machine in his garage and rowed for ten minutes on his own accord because he wanted to. At this point, he took his exercise regimen over and began to own his physical fitness. He was at the point where he could set goals on his own, push himself, and create a plan that would get him back to the fitness level he once had.

Human beings are not light switches. We do not flip off and on and simply start new habits or stop old ones. We have to ease into change to make it stick and be successful. When it comes to fitness, we ease into it. We do the same for nutrition.

Nutrition and Hydration

We are what we eat. Many first responders eat poorly and fuel their bodies with caffeine, sugar, and fat. Granted, some shifts are not conducive to proper nutrition at the right times because the tempo simply does not allow for healthy eating. The key is to eat right as often as you can and certainly when you are off duty.

Some of my customers have nutritionists who visit with the first responders. This is one of the most progressive and effective ways to care for public safety personnel. I have observed first responders interact with nutritionists and it is an absolute delight to watch them ask questions, learn about better options, set nutrition goals, and create plans that coincide with their fitness goals. This is an incredible opportunity, and I have never heard a first responder say they did not benefit from time with a nutritionist.

The other important aspect here is hydration. Public safety professionals are mass consumers of energy drinks, despite the plethora of studies showing how unhealthy they are. When I speak at conferences, I tell first responders that one of the best things they can do for their health is to quit energy drinks. I always get the look of death from at least five people in the room, but seriously, who wants to deal with such things as gout, sleep impairment, cardiovascular issues, and nervousness?

I previously stated that human beings are not light switches. This concept applies when making nutritional changes. I ask first responders to refrain from crash diets and unrealistic, sudden changes to their normal eating patterns. Instead, I ask them to simply take two bites of what they know they should not eat off their plates, and add two bites of what they know they should eat onto their plates. The same applies to energy drinks. Sudden withdrawal will make anyone feel awful, so I ask first responders to taper off slowly. The key here is to ensure success and lasting change.

Sleep and Rest

The job of being a first responder involves being available twenty-four hours a day. Shift work, rotating shifts, swing shifts, night shifts, twenty-four-hour shifts, forty-eight-hour shifts—you name it, first responders do them all. They defy sleep, power through the brain's need to sleep, and keep going. No wonder first responders complain about how little and how poorly they sleep, even when they are off.

Circadian Rhythm Sleep Disorder (CRSD) is an extremely prevalent problem for first responders. CRSD is a sleep disorder in which one's internal sleep/wake clock is disrupted, resulting in disturbed sleep and daytime fatigue. Because our bodies run in sync to a twenty-four-hour circadian rhythm, the discrepancy between emergency services work and the body's natural desire to go to sleep, stay asleep, and be awake based on periods of darkness and light causes CRSD. Circadian Rhythm Sleep Disorder can lead to insomnia, medical problems, cognitive impairment, mood disturbances, and interpersonal problems.

Another aspect of emergency work is the constant production of adrenaline, glucose, and cortisol in fight-

or-flight responses. First responders may have several limbic system activations in each shift. They may be existing in a constant state of fight or flight throughout each period while on duty. And at the end of the shift comes the adrenaline dump, which means that by the time first responders walk through the front door of their home, they can barely put one foot in front of the other.

Paying attention to sleep difficulties is important for first responders. The brain and the body use sleep to restore, heal, process trauma, reproduce and repair cells, solidify information that was not ingrained during the day, and to preserve memories.

To improve sleep in my patients, I will always start with the most conservative approach. I recommend that first responders keep a consistent schedule when they are off duty and go to bed at the same time every night. I also recommend that they keep a consistent routine at bedtime to cue their brains into understanding that it is time to go to sleep. My patients and I work on sleep hygiene, such as decluttering their room and making it cool, dark, and quiet. We also work on reducing the use of cell phones and tablets at bedtime. Bright screens have been shown to stimulate the brain to wake up. I recommend exercise as a great way to improve sleep. I highlight the importance of naps and minimizing alcohol intake before bed. My patients typically use melatonin when they can't sleep, or some sort of antihistamine that will cause drowsiness.

If none of this works, I ask my patients to have a

conversation with their medical doctor. I encourage first responders to consider sleep studies and treatments for sleep disorders with prescription medications as the very last option. If they are given a prescription medication for sleep, I strongly encourage that they only take it occasionally when they must get rest but just cannot fall asleep. The majority of sleep medicines are full of depressants (this is why they knock people out) and are extremely habit forming.

In the aftermath of a large-scale traumatic event, a police officer told me that she was given a prescription medication to help her sleep. Eight months after the incident, she had gone from taking one pill a night to taking two, with a delay in onset of sleep of four hours. She later sent me an email telling me she was going through the withdrawal process from the medication and was absolutely miserable. She stated she wished she had never started taking it and that her doctor had recommended counseling instead.

Alcohol

Alcohol is the gas on the fire when it comes to mental and physical health problems.

For most first responders, it starts with a happy hour or a simple cocktail at home to relax after a particularly rough shift. Repeated over time, it becomes habitual behavior, with increasing amounts and frequency of alcohol use. Before they realize it, some first responders have developed a dependency on alcohol or are even abusing it.

When first responders are healing from post-traumatic stress disorder, I am so relieved when they tell me that they don't drink at all or that they drink occasionally or socially. PTSD cannot be mitigated if a patient drinks while we do to the difficult work of treating trauma. The bottom line is this: if there is alcohol abuse or dependence, we will have to climb that mountain before we can truly address the case of trauma.

Alcohol consumption is a very personal choice. If a first responder realizes they need help, I strongly encourage them to tackle it however they can. Whether they see a therapist, go to support groups, attend an intensive outpatient program, or even go inpatient, it will be worth it to quit.

I recently had a patient who wanted to treat his trauma from military deployments to Iraq and his public safety career. He was drinking a fifth of vodka each night. He agreed to taper, and he actually quit drinking in three weeks. He reported feeling so much better, it caused him to get truly motivated to conquer his trauma and improve his life. After he quit drinking, his time in therapy was accelerated, because with a clear mind he was able to process his traumas quickly. I discharged a completely different person than the one who came to my office—an incredible transformation.

Check-ups and Labs

Because being a first responder is inherently demanding and stressful both physically and mentally, it is essential to the health of all public safety professionals to see their primary care physician at least once a year and to address any changes to their baseline health. A standard check-up is not comprehensive enough, however, for most first responders.

Fight or flight is a common occurrence for first responders. They frequently exist in this state constantly and chronically. I jokingly refer to first responders as chemical nightmares due to the voluminous amounts of glucocorticoids produced during most shifts. While this becomes the norm for first responders, it is not the norm at all for the general public. Many physicians might not understand what their first responder patients are going through physically, shift after shift. Therefore, I encourage first responders to request extra labs to assure that they are healthy.

When a first responder describes fatigue, poor motivation, little interest in the things they normally enjoy, lethargy and apathy, I refer them to their doctor for a blood test. While this might sound like depression to most mental health professionals, based on what first responders go through by the nature of the work they do, I want to see lab results first. I ask first responders to get their thyroids checked, along with vitamin D and cortisol. I also ask male first responders to get their testosterone checked. The chemistry of chronic fight or flight can create significant problems in first responders. I have known three first responders who have absolutely bottomed out on cortisol production. I have met many first responders with the testosterone levels of eighty-five-year-old men. All of these issues will make anyone want to climb inside a hole and never come out!

Considerations for Loved Ones

Holding down the fort at home when your public safety loved one is away for long shifts can be difficult. Managing the demands of home, your own career, and that of your public safety loved one can be monumentally difficult. When your first responder is at work and they call home, they typically sound great. They are often witty, energized, and happy, because the chemistry of the first responder during a shift involves a lot of adrenaline. Because the brain is designed to let off this response when the shift is over, your first responder is actually going through an adrenaline withdrawal by the time they get home. This is akin to a physical withdrawal from a high. When they enter your home, what you experience is this withdrawal—they are deflated, tired, irritated, withdrawn, and sometimes short-tempered, and it is common for family members to ask their first responders, "Why are you so happy at work and so angry at home?"

Please understand that this is nothing your first responder is doing on purpose. It has everything to do with the mental and physical letdown after a shift requiring vigilance. The key here is for both of you to know how to manage this situation. Whether your first responder needs to go to bed immediately or to take a nap or to have a mindless decompression period, work this out with them.

I try to do family education days for my customers as often as I can. I once explained to a group of firefighters' spouses that after a forty-eight-hour shift, when they walk in the front door and are going through the adrenaline dump, they have to take a nap. I explained to the spouses that if their loved one's shift ends on a Saturday morning and they are met with a "Honey Do" list along with seventeen errands to run, culminating in a four-year old's birthday party at the end of the day, their firefighter would be acting even worse than the four-year-old kids at the party. One of the wives exclaimed, "That's exactly right. This explains everything!" Later that month I received a text from her husband, thanking me for explaining things to her. They were able to work out a better way to approach those first days off and it made a huge difference.

A mantra to remember would be: when in doubt, slow down, communicate, and breathe. Stay focused on attacking the problem and not each other.

Chapter Four
Mental Health

Voices, In my head again
Baiting me in a war I can't win
I can hear them now
Trapped in a game inside my own skin
I don't know myself anymore
They're pulling me under
Voices, Voices

"Voices" by Motionless in White

Mental health and public safety have been like oil to water since I began my career twenty-seven years ago. Throughout most of my time as a professional, the field of emergency services has largely associated any sort of mental health issue with signs of weakness and has viewed receiving help as an indicator of one's inability to do the job. While this could not be further from the truth, it is exactly the attitude I have fought against for a long time.

Fortunately, the tide is turning. The field of emergency services is at critical mass. The suicide, divorce, attrition, and burnout rates have increased so significantly that leadership in emergency services can no longer afford to ignore mental health issues.

I have stated throughout my entire career that we cannot expect to insert first responders into the worst situations repeatedly and not expect them to struggle at some point. It is human nature to be impacted by violence, abuse, suffering, carnage, and evil. First responders are not robots. They are not sociopaths. They are going to be impacted. This is a normal process.

In my book *First Responder Resilience: Caring for Public Servants*, I outlined elements of a good mental health plan for first responders. The best plans include truly confidential, ongoing help by clinicians who are competent with first responders, as well as services that are not cost-prohibitive. I also outlined the educational components for first responder mental health and resilience, which are essential in teaching first responders how to care for themselves and how to ask for help if they need it. What I want to focus on here is the mental health of each first responder and the implications of getting help.

Getting Help

Making the call to ask for help is likely one of the hardest things a first responder will do. So often, as I take calls from first responders, I can hear the apprehension in their voices. I assure them it is okay to ask for help, that everyone struggles at some point. By the time most first responders ask for assistance, they are really hurting.

Finding the right therapist is similar to buying a new car—you might have to test drive a few to find the right one. The first thing to do is to check them out—look at their websites and check out their specialties. The best therapists are typically highly specialized, so if you are looking for someone to help you with trauma and find someone who lists twenty-five specialties that include trauma, you might need to keep looking. If possible, interview them on the phone. Ask them about their experiences with emergency services and your topics of concern. If you sit down with a clinician and have a sense that you cannot trust or open up to that person, it is important to keep looking. Trust your instincts.

When you attend therapy, you do not have to tolerate therapists who forget your appointments, who show up late, or who confuse you with other patients. You also don't have to tolerate therapists who have no idea what you do, or those who are shocked by what you say. If this happens, it's time to move on.

When you begin therapy, you should expect to set goals, along with objectives to reach those goals. Homework is part of the change process, but the amount of homework should only be as much as you can easily accomplish. Because you are a consumer and you have patient's rights, you are allowed to veto or disagree with what your therapist assigns. This is a collaborative process and you have a say. The point is, you should stay in control of your treatment.

Creating Change

The main reasons first responders seek help are trauma (see Chapter Five) and a sense of loss of control. When public safety professionals reach out, their usual coping mechanisms are failing, and they don't know what to do. They are so used to fixing everything—because their job requires it—that they are often in disbelief that they need help themselves. Whatever the issue, with the right commitment and attitude, enough change can be made to either resolve an issue or at least bring about change and consequently a sense of relief.

As first responders begin therapy, the blood work mentioned in Chapter Three is essential. It gives us a baseline for your current physical status. In the mental health world, a prerequisite for diagnosing any mental health disorder is to first rule out all physiological disorders. Too often, therapists forget or overlook this fact. They see things in terms of mental health. Think of it as someone whose only tool is a hammer. Everything starts to look like a nail to him sooner or later.

I once saw a police officer who complained of anxiety. He told me that he did not understand why he was so anxious, because he loves his job and loves his family. Life was good, and he could not figure out why he was so anxious. I sent him to a physician to have his blood checked. The results were low testosterone, low cortisol, low vitamin D, and hyperthyroidism. All of this manifested as anxiety. His doctor called him back for more testing immediately. This police officer, it turns out, did not need me. Imagine the time we would have wasted and the frustration he would have experienced if I treated him for anxiety in a counseling realm.

If blood work comes back normal, then we know we can move on to psychological care. Together we create the plan of attack—goals, objectives to reach those goals, and ultimately a path ahead. We work on letting go of anger, overcoming adversity, moving through grief and loss, overcoming PTSD, forgiving others, forgiving yourself, family dynamics, or whatever the first responder brings to the sessions. Once first responders feel comfortable in a therapeutic setting, they frequently choose to tackle more issues than they initially presented, which means that they trust the process and can feel the benefits.

Brain Health Equals Heart Health

The connection between the mind and body is remarkable. There is no doubt that poor mental health impacts physical health and vice versa. Whether you start healing and improving one or the other, or both at the same time, just start.

I had a sheriff's deputy who was seeing me for multiple work-related traumas. He was skeptical about

EMDR (Eye Movement Desensitization and Reprocessing) until he completed it. This deputy experienced such significant relief from the process, he started to change his habits.

During his first week after EMDR, he told me he cut his alcohol consumption in half. He did this because he no longer had to numb himself to go to sleep, and he was sleeping better. The following week he cut his alcohol even further and he started going back to the gym. From this point forward, there was no stopping the deputy's success. He continues to set goals as he improves himself every day.

As a clinician, I can encourage, ask, and even beg first responders to trust in the process. I completely understand that because of my credentials, there is still apprehension for many first responders to get help. Hearing it from other first responders means so much more and carries a significantly heavier weight. More than half of the patients who call my office tell me that a Peer Support Team member encouraged them to call. The credibility is there, and it is important. In this book I have recruited three patients to provide an account of their journey of getting help. I choose to finish this chapter with Bess's story because I know it means so much more than anything I can write.

Bess's Story: Is This Real?

When I walked out of the dispatch center that day, I had

no idea that I wasn't going back, or that I had taken my last 911 call after thirty-three years in emergency services. It was just foggy. The departure, the unfamiliarity, walking out, the drive to where? It was all very foggy. Where was I going, what was I supposed to be doing? I had never felt like this before. I've taken hundreds, even thousands, a gazillion calls in my career. Was this the worst call? Who determines that? Certainly not me, I'm not the victim. The victim is the only one who knows that, right?

The anxiety, the panic, the uneasiness, the uncertainty, an overwhelming sadness, the depression, the isolation, the memory problems, distortion in my thoughts, and now insomnia: are they real? I believed that these things could be real for other people, but not for me. I've always been in control, or at least I thought so. Control, ha! Did I no longer have control? The anxiety—is this real, how could that be possible? Insomnia, pssfffft, just go to sleep, just wake up, do what you have to do. And my mind and my memory started playing tricks on me. Was I crazy? Was I losing my mind? These things couldn't be real.

July 9 at 17:50, the 911 call, the murders, the horrendous murders, not one or two died, BUT SIX. Did you hear me? SIX family members dead. Are you kidding me? This is not real. This is unfathomable. Seven people were shot in the head by a relative, and there was only one lone survivor. And SHE, she called me for help. Did I help her? I don't know; did I? I didn't even have time to wrap my head around any of that, while on my foggy drive from the communication center to the debriefing at the fire station, I saw him, the shooter. He drove right in front of me in the police pursuit while I was stopped at a red light. He drove through that very intersection where I sat in my car; he was there, in his car in front of me. What just happened? Was any of this real?

According to worker's comp, it was not even tangible that I had PTSD. They have a really hard time coding it and placing it in a so-called category. There are no broken bones, or injured backs, or obvious visible signs of injury. There are only hopes and prayers that they don't leave you out in the cold alone to figure it all out on your own. I learned along the way that I was one of the lucky ones, though it didn't always feel that way. I had a pretty good support system, mostly.

Along came all the debriefings, and there were many, all pretty good, some better than others. There were many caring, understanding, compassionate, some knowledgeable, some not, counselors, critical-incident persons, chaplains, many prayers, and preachers, even an actual therapist in the mix. It was helpful, it was a start. So, the therapy began. There was that first really bad, chastised complimentary session with the boss's therapist friend. Well, let's just say, not so much. That was a pretty bad experience, with quite a few more to come in this journey. There were the compassionate, really caring ones, but they really didn't have a chance to get the momentum going, not enough time to help, their time was limited and dictated by the rules; one was EAP (Employee Assistance Program) and another one was a temporary volunteer. Where do you go from there? I was alone in my mind, I isolated myself, I had lots of time to think and think and think, I felt hopeless and helpless, I felt frustrated by some of the help I was or wasn't getting. I went through and felt so many things, especially in the earlier stages of my journey. I lost so much time, it just passed, it just disappeared; time was fleeting and standing still at the same time. And there were all these stages or phases, my own way of organizing it in my mind, trying to figure out my level of wellness—was I better, was I worse? I've heard that tough guys don't need help, or don't ask for help, or they're afraid of the stigma so they don't reach out. I was once one of those people in my younger years, early in my career, the John Wayne types we called it back in the 80s, just pick up your boot straps and get back to work. Well I'm here to tell you, I never felt like this before, not having control, not being able to tell myself what I was matter-of-fact going to do, and how I was going to just cope with it. I did not have control; *this was real*. It's hard to swallow, shame, guilt, embarrassment, belittlement, neglect of myself and things around me, not just neglect but literally incapable of accomplishing something, I couldn't just talk it away, it wasn't leaving me.

When I wasn't isolating myself, I made attempts in the real world. That might include avoiding the route of my departure from work that day, and any roads related, like the intersection where I saw the shooter. However, in retrospect, I would drive through the neighborhood and drive by the house of the murders many times; taking pictures, making notes, sketching, pondering, even eating lunch in the neighborhood park. Or sometimes I would drive to the cemetery and sit on the family memorial bench surrounded by six graves and cry and pray. I was a mess. I often sat in my car in many parking lots, sometimes for hours, unsuccessfully attempting to go places or get things done. I couldn't even get out at Walgreen's to run in and grab a package of cough drops. Watching people all around going in and out and in and out, and I could not even get out of my vehicle. Once I had my six-year-old niece with me, we pulled into the grocery store parking lot and parked. I had my grocery list; I thought surely having her with me would prove easier this time. And we sat there for a long time. She was buckled into her car seat in the back, I sat in the driver seat. She just pondered me, she was confused by me, she wanted to know, "What are we doing?" I could not respond to her; I just cried. And when I stopped, I told her that we were leaving, that we were not going in the store. It was pretty overwhelming. Although she was only six, I felt embarrassed and defeated. I was trying to be normal.

Therapy and more therapy and more and more therapy. One bad group and one good group. One psychiatrist, and one psychiatrist too many, I might add. I call him Dr. Coo-Coo—someday I'll tell that story, it was bad! But the therapists, oh, the therapists, there were so many. Some really, really good ones. I prayed a lot: "Dear God, am I in the right place, is this where I'm supposed to be, will this last forever and when will I be cured?"

There were one-on-one talks, small groups, big groups, pow-wows. Then the bio-feedback mumbo-jumbo, which might be legit, if it wasn't improperly labeled by Dr. Coo-Coo, who just wanted other ways to bill workers' compensation for additional sessions. I had some pretty good therapy going on with one group of therapists before Dr. Coo-Coo bullied me away from them. And that is where I had some exposure to EMDR, by a therapist "with training" and "no experience" in EMDR, and she took a stab at it; it did not go well. I know you have to start somewhere, but it wasn't with me, it was all wrong. And prior to that "one time" with her, I had a small, rushed dose of EMDR at a critical incident seminar. It was good, it was positive, but it felt rushed, it felt like a "drive-by," and it must have been just that for me, because it didn't really stick.

I tried to stay diligent in my own care from day one, because I was so foggy. I kept everything: notes, files, papers, business cards, sticky notes, and anything else that helped me remember. I put them all in a file and a binder and a box. I had to, because my memory was playing tricks on me; it still does. Could be old age, but I never had this before. Oh, I didn't even mention all the

Code Four: Surviving and Thriving in Public Safety

physical ails that came along with my PTSD; that's another whole story for another time. When I was referred to another therapist or doctor because one doctor moved her practice, or a therapist moved out of state, or because of an insurance referral, or because I relocated from one city to another, in my diligence to find a good fit for my needs, I would ask, "Do you have someone who specializes in PTSD" or someone who is "familiar with emergency services" or "I'll take someone familiar with war veterans' experience if it's the closest I can get."

Recently I received a recommendation, not just once but actually for the second or third time, to this particular therapist in my relocated city. At first, I had not really tried to get into their office, for various reasons: location, timing, insurance, my worthiness, etc. However, I eventually lucked out. I got an appointment; I was in. I met with my assigned therapist, and I found out that they offered EMDR. I believed in it by what I knew about it, I just felt like it had not quite been administered properly. And here it was, my choice, my timing, when I was ready. I was hopeful, I was nervous, somewhat apprehensive and a little anxious, but I was ready. So we did it, I did it. It was crazy, like a fast-forwarding movie. I saw so many things, memories, not just the murder incident, but other things. I saw pictures in my mind, other cases in my career, old cases, from years and years ago. And I saw other incidents in my life; it was like slow-motion running fast through my mind. That must be an oxymoron, ha! It was exhausting, and overwhelming, and mind boggling, and invigorating at the same time. A very stressful headache followed, and I'm not usually prone to have headaches. This made it more apparent to me. But more importantly than all of that, I had a strong sense of relief. Some sort of clarity, and I felt a release of being stuck in a therapeutic rut, so to speak. I can't even explain it. I'll let the experts do that. It has been a long time coming. It feels like a breakthrough. Wow, EMDR, I am grateful.

Air Evac Lifeteam Peer Support

Austin Travis County EMS Peer Support

Customs and Border Protection Air and Marine Operations Peer Support

Avondale Fire Peer Support

Eastern Arizona Peer Support

Leander Fire Peer Support

Leander, Round Rock, and Cedar Park Fire Peer Support Training

Multiple Peer Support Teams from Texas

Williamson County Sheriff's Peer Support Training

NYPD Peer Support Reunion (All were active after 9.11)

PHI Air Medical Peer Support

Pinal County Peer Support

Teton Interagency Peer Support

Chapter Five

Trauma

If I fall again, will it be the end?
I know it's wrong
You think I'm strong, but I just pretend
Is it taking over?
Will it bury me?
Or will clarity become the cure for my disease?

"Disease" by Beartooth

When addressing trauma, many of my first responders say things like, "At least I didn't have to go through Fallujah and kick in door after door." My veterans who come in to address trauma say things like, "At least I only had to do this for a year, not like cops and firefighters who have to do this for twenty or more years." What I tell all of them: trauma is trauma.

Whether first responders experience a bad call, are subjected to violence, or experience an absolutely horrific event that completely overwhelms them, trauma is trauma. It ultimately gets stored in the brain the same way, it manifests itself with the same intrusive ugliness, and ultimately either gets processed and dealt with or it does not, depending on the aftermath for each first responder.

This chapter is about how I approach trauma. No response is ever perfect, but I do believe in doing what works, in doing no harm, and ultimately helping restore the hearts and minds of public servants.

PTSD: The Beginning

Post-traumatic stress disorder is the end result of being exposed to a stress trauma so severe that it is beyond human coping capacity. Not everyone exposed to a traumatic event will develop post-traumatic stress disorder. PTSD is a highly individualized reaction to an extreme stressor that usually involves the actual or perceived threat of death to a person or to someone else in close proximity to that person. While every first responder has their own individual threshold for stress, that level generally increases over time (this is the "been there, done that" approach that seasoned first responders have). Everyone has their own individual point beyond which they will become overwhelmed. No matter how long a person has been active in public safety, there is some type of event that, given the right circumstances, could be beyond their coping capacity.

Trauma starts with the five senses: what first responders see, hear, taste, touch, and smell. When an event is not a problem for the individual first responder, the information is transmitted from the frontal lobe of the brain and, in essence, "downloaded" into memory, where it is either stored or deleted according to the event's relevance. With trauma, however, the frontal lobe of the brain acts as a screener and does not allow the information to be processed across the synapses and downloaded into memory. Because the event is interpreted by the brain as too abnormal, traumatic, or horrific, the frontal lobe will capture the information and store it to deal with later.

When an event is over and a first responder attempts to go back to their normal routine, the frontal lobe will begin to attempt to address the information that it has captured. This is the brain's way of trying to figure out how to interpret the information and download it into memory. The timeframe for this to begin can be hours, days, weeks, or even months after an incident and usually occurs as the post-incident numbing wears off. At this point, the first responder will become aware that things do not seem right and consequently becomes uncomfortable with what their mind is doing to them.

Where We Start:
Immediate Intervention and Prevention

Immediate crisis intervention through peer support has been a significant mechanism for preventing and mitigating problems occurring in the aftermath of trauma. I train and maintain Peer Support Teams and consider them an extension of my practice. I have witnessed over and over again how properly trained and guided Peer Support Teams save lives of first responders.

The first step in the aftermath of someone's trauma is to start with the Maslow's Hierarchy of Needs pyramid. Availability of basic needs—such as food, water, clothing, and shelter—is a necessity. Peer Support Teams that start here will never fail first responders. It starts with the simple act of handing someone a bottle of water because after a fight-or-flight response, public safety personnel are severely dehydrated and numb. Because they are numb, they have no idea how thirsty they are until they take the first sip of water.

From there we consider what each first responder needs next. Perhaps it's some sweatpants and a fresh shirt because a uniform is contaminated or is now considered evidence. Next, it may be a ride home, a meal, helping get the kids to or from daycare, or getting in touch with family members. I train Peer Support Team members to identify these needs and assist in any way they can.

From this point on I encourage Peer Support Team members to remain present and continue to assist. One of my teams recently responded to a horrific law enforcement incident. They noticed that the officers involved were not eating. When the team took the officers to breakfast the following day, the officers assured them that they were not hungry. Within minutes of smelling food, they were famished.

What is happening at this point is the impacted personnel are beginning to return to their normal level of functioning. While it seems so simple, this process is circumventing the alternative, which only serves to worsen the trauma. Imagine the alternative, which happens all too often: first responders go home, stare at four walls, mentally beat themselves up, don't hydrate, don't eat, and instead get intoxicated. The next day is no better and the day after is even worse. Yet, somehow we expect first responders to come back for their next shift ready to perform as though nothing is wrong.

The simple act of sharing a meal, going for a walk, working out together, seeing a movie, or tending to daily needs gives first responders the ability to begin the reset. Encouraging healthy, relaxing, and normal activities signals the brain that it is okay to come off a fight-or-flight mode and begin to reset.

As peer support continues to walk with first responders on their darkest days, the rapport and trust that is built lends itself to a good outlet for public safety personnel to begin to share their stories. But this only happens when they are ready. In the first forty-eight to seventy-two hours, an event is a blur. All the details cannot yet be recalled and events are out of order, because at the time of the event—in the fight-or-flight response—the prefrontal cortex shuts down. The prefrontal cortex is the portion of the brain responsible for thinking, reasoning, analyzing, decision-making, logic, and memory management. It can take a several days before the prefrontal cortex fully turns back on.

In the first two to three days, Peer Support Teams are trained to listen and assess where the first responder is in terms of their cognition because the first two days are characterized by high distractibility and forgetfulness. My teams typically help their first responders make lists of things to do and people to call. Peer support drives them where they need to go and notices such things as pets needing to be let out or fed. They notice the fact that the front door is left unlocked or that there are no groceries in the refrigerator. An extremely important role first responders play at this point is advocating a delay in report writing or official statements being made. There is no reason to ask someone for the most important legal statement of a lifetime when their brain has not yet returned to full capacity.

As time progresses, team members are there to listen to their first responders. The story will come out when the impacted person is ready. There is no rush. It might be all at once and it might be in bits and pieces. Peer support is there to listen, normalize, validate, educate, and encourage healing. They are never there to judge, criticize, or question their first responders. Sometimes peer support is the only person or group of people who do not do any of these things. I truly believe we all need someone in our corner to back us up when things are not good.

As time progresses, the brain tells us that it is resolving the trauma or it isn't. For my customers, as I train them on trauma and stress, I let them know about timelines for preventive care. I give my first responders the following parameters: at one-week post-incident, I want everyone to experience some fading. In other words, the sights, smells, and sounds that replayed over and over in their minds during the first three days should begin to dissipate or fade. At two weeks post-incident, I want the sights, smells, and sounds "banked" in their long-term memory. In other words, the nightmares, constant replay, and intrusive images should have stopped. I explain that the experience is as though the event is really fading. If someone asks a question or there is a news story, it is normal to think about it, but other than that, the event is banked in long-term memory. If at two weeks a significant amount of fading has not occurred, I want first responders to seek help immediately.

What Happens Next: Trauma Treatment

Whether the trauma is recent or not, I strongly encourage first responders to get help if they are struggling. The course of treatment is typically faster if help is sought quickly, but it is never too late to get help.

The field of trauma treatment has advanced greatly in the past twenty-seven years. When I was in graduate school, trauma was a three-hour lecture. Now, there are entire tracts through graduate schools focusing on trauma work. We have evidence-based interventions that mitigate post-traumatic stress disorder very effectively.

Many first responders have been able to combat their PTSD without any problem. The key is to get help when help is needed.

When first responders see therapists for trauma, it is a good idea to interview them, get an assessment of their experience and comfort level, and to find out what treatment modalities they use. Research these modalities and make sure you are comfortable with them, with the therapist you have chosen, and with the general atmosphere of the therapist's office.

In 1995 I was trained in EMDR—Eye Movement Desensitization and Reprocessing. This is a technique designed to allow the brain to unlock the traumatic images stored in the frontal lobe and download them into long-term memory, where they belong. While we all have bad memories, we have control of those memories, and they don't trigger and haunt us all day long. Trauma that is stored in the frontal lobe triggers constantly. By moving the images to the portion of the brain where they should be stored, a significant amount of relief is achieved. The thing I love about EMDR is that it taps into the brain's ability to heal itself, and it does this quickly.

I have used EMDR to combat trauma in hundreds of first responders and veterans. Whether I use it for older trauma that has existed for a while or on fresh trauma in a preventive realm, the results are incredible. I see people restored to their normal resilience almost every day.

I typically couple EMDR with progressive desensitization, which means we go back out to the scene where it happened. We get back in the helicopter or tackle whatever situation has caused the trauma. I use Peer Support Team members to do this portion of the care as often as I can, fully realizing that a first responder patient would rather revisit the scene with a battle buddy than with a therapist. By doing progressive desensitization, we remove the anxiety and the bite from going to the place where the trauma occurred for the first time. I absolutely make sure my patients are ready for this treatment. And by the time trauma treatment is done, they are usually excited to go conquer this final step.

Group Interventions

During and after trauma, I strongly discourage group interventions that compel first responders to speak. Sitting in a circle with a group of public safety personnel, asking them to recall and recount on the trauma, runs a high risk of re-traumatizing first responders.

If group interventions are done, I do encourage things like breakfast at the station for first responders, with an opportunity to discuss the event if they would like to. I encourage very casual, low-key interventions that are not mandatory, probing, or invasive.

In my book *First Responder Resilience: Caring for Public Servants*, I presented the TEN FOUR model, which is designed to manage group interventions effectively. The Peer Support Team provides TEN: triage, educate, and normalize. This means triaging the impacted personnel to assure those in each group had a similar exposure to the event and educating first responders about normal reactions to stress and stress management strategies. The impacted first responders then do the FOUR: free discussion, organize thoughts, understand the big picture, and restore resilience. This means they have free discussion, they begin to put the pieces of the puzzle back together, they see the event in terms of the big picture, and they work to get back to normal as quickly as possible. I have consistently found that first responders respond positively to casual, easygoing, and low-key interventions consistent with the TEN FOUR model.

Allowing First Responders Space and Time

Anyone who has been in the field for any length of time knows that sometimes, for the preservation of sanity, certain types of calls just need to be avoided for a while. For instance, when returning from a bad shift into a busy home with multiple family obligations. Or when there is no time to process a bad call. Or simply not knowing what to make of a call. This will require more time.

One night while on duty in the emergency room where I worked for ten years, EMS encoded with two people from a house fire—one adult and one pediatric patient. The patients we received were a mother and her six-year-old son. As EMS gave their report, they whispered that the father and the daughter of this family had died in the fire. I spoke to the mother quickly to obtain family phone numbers just before she was intubated. I went into her son's room and introduced myself to him. The next thing he did shocked all of us. He took my hand and said, "Tania, I know my father and sister are dead, and I just don't know how my mom and I are going to get through this." The entire treatment team left the room quickly to hide their tears while I stood there and choked back my own tears to console this beautiful child. The remaining nine hours of the shift were the longest I have ever experienced.

Driving home in the morning, a friend asked how my shift went. All I said was, "Not good." He asked if I wanted to talk about it and all I could say was, "Not even a little bit." It was the kind of night shift where the scrubs were tossed into the washing machine immediately and washed twice. Six months later, I was finally able to talk about the event.

Having space and time to let things settle in your mind, taking the time to get some rest and get a good workout in, going home and hugging your kids and kissing them about fifty times are excellent forms of therapy. Taking this time is essential to recovery. It opens the door to being ready to process bad calls safely and effectively.

Special Considerations: Survivor High

"If that doesn't kill me, what will? One side of my helmet was crushed. I walked away from the wreck without a scratch. So what did I do? I bought a faster motorcycle!"

In public safety there are traumas and traumatic calls, and then there are the life-threatening traumas defined by horror well beyond the norm. These are the sorts of events where first responders face their most difficult and dangerous challenges. They are the "near death," "could have died," "can't believe I survived" moments that define a career, that change a person. In my twenty-seven years of practice, I have focused on "cleaning up trauma" and other complications that result from events like this. Lately, however, I have added another feature to the care I give emergency services personnel—addressing what I refer to as Survivor High Syndrome.

In a recent peer support training with the United States Border Patrol, I described the Survivor High Syndrome, which manifests itself in increased thrill-seeking and risk-taking behavior as demonstrated by first responders *after* a near-death situation. Asking the audience about it, I was floored to see all forty-five nodding their heads in agreement. I asked the class for some examples. Incident after incident was recounted by agents as they discussed what they had witnessed assisting fellow agents. From buying faster motorcycles to discounting safety while on the line, to engaging in extra-marital affairs, my peer support class that day shared some incredibly dangerous risk-taking behavior.

When we, as human beings, whether for a brief moment or for prolonged periods of time, perceive that we might lose our life, such an event can change us. It is a red flag for the onset of post-traumatic stress disorder.

Whether engaging in risky behavior to tempt fate, playing with the limitations of life, or recreating the thrill and rush of survival, the bottom line is that these behaviors are extremely dangerous. First responders are not likely to mention their "highs" to Peer Support Team members or clinicians. They may not even realize that they are engaging in such behavior. When I asked if she was experiencing Survivor High Syndrome, a flight nurse told me after an aviation incident that she was taking curves too fast and was testing the limits of her motorcycle. Advised of the danger, she promptly grounded herself from her motorcycle for two weeks. Other times, first responders might not mention it because they are enjoying the thrill and are hooked on the rush. Without realizing it, they are placing their physical and mental health in danger, which is the worst-case scenario after already sustaining trauma associated with a separate incident.

The solution is education, awareness, and open discussion with our first responders. Having this conversation with first responders is an important part of the early aftermath. The last thing anyone wants is for a first responder to further complicate their life and pay the ultimate price in an act of thrill seeking with inevitable results.

Special Considerations: Survival Guilt

Recently I did EMDR on a combat veteran who is now a police officer. He has been to hell and back and has nothing left to prove. The struggle has been real, but he is resilient and committed to healing and leading a very productive life. One of the traumas he processed in his EMDR session was the death of a fellow soldier. The two were close—they had joined at the same time, trained together, deployed together, and were solid friends. My patient was promoted. The logical choice was to move him to another unit. Instead, his friend was moved—shortly before his death. My patient suffered from tremendous Survivor Guilt—the unbelievably painful aftermath of surviving when someone you care about is killed. "Why me?" he asked. "He had a wife and children and I was single," he explained. We hear this all too often.

I asked him to continue to process his Survivor Guilt in EMDR and when he was ready to hear it, I explained to him that emotions, including Survivor Guilt, are logical, predictable, and understandable. An emotion is the result of information—the who, what, where, when, and how—and an individual's interpretation of such information. When we look at what has happened to us and how we interpret it, our reactions make sense.

As we heal, our interpretations and thus our reactions change. My patient asked how Survivor Guilt lessens, fully understanding that it will probably never go away completely. Admittedly, I wish I had a magic eraser for this kind of pain.

We discussed time as a healer, resolving trauma that changes your perspective, and the ability to forgive oneself. After another set of EMDR, he addressed the impact of Survivor Guilt on his current decision-making and actions. He began to understand how it permeates his life. I asked him to consider that his Survivor Guilt has been like a bowling ball chained to his leg. He drags it everywhere he goes, and it severely impacts his life. I handed him a stress ball and asked him to rethink his Survivor Guilt. I asked him to take the Survivor Guilt from a bowling ball to the stress ball: "Embrace it, look at it, acknowledge it, stick it in your pocket, and on bad days throw it against the wall as many times as you need to. While we can't erase it, let's manage it." My patient walked out of the office carrying the stress ball with a very different demeanor and outlook.

I would ask anyone who is struggling with Survivor Guilt to allow yourself to heal. Get help. Take your guilt from bowling ball to stress ball. Please don't keep dragging the bowling ball any farther because it will take you down.

Code Four: Surviving and Thriving in Public Safety

Special Considerations: Anger

Anger is an umbrella emotion. It covers up other emotions, such as pain, fear, sorrow, sadness, grief, and vulnerability. The emotions we don't want to feel and certainly don't want to show are covered up with anger. This keeps us safe. Anger can be toxic. It can destroy relationships and careers.

I also consider anger a tool. Used properly, anger can lead us to incredible achievements and growth. I tell first responders to use their anger in a way that is productive and healing. "Make it make you better" is how I explain this to first responders.

Directed properly, anger helps us achieve and accomplish so much. Run the 5K, the 10K, the marathon. Go the next level in CrossFit. Form a nonprofit that helps veterans or first responders. Volunteer to help foster children. Whatever you choose, take your anger and make it productive.

My favorite example of productive anger is John Walsh of the TV show *America's Most Wanted.* Mr. Walsh's son, Adam, was abducted and murdered. I can only guess that for a period of time Mr. Walsh struggled with what to do with his anger. Then he created a TV show that caught really bad criminals by the thousands. Out of a tragedy comes good. Just remember to make it make you better.

Special Considerations for Loved Ones

Loving a first responder who goes through trauma is a bumpy ride. It is normal to be afraid, angry, and impatient to just get back to normal as you attempt to help your first responder overcome a trauma. Please understand that it may take a while for your loved one to open up about what has happened. They, in turn, worry about traumatizing their loved ones if they share these types of events.

Vicarious trauma is when loved ones, by nature and virtue of what happens to the first responder, are also traumatized. Whether you see the event on the news, hear about it from your first responder or someone else, or simply see and feel the impact on your loved one, it is normal to develop vicarious trauma. When this happens, you might experience some of the same symptoms that your first responder is experiencing. Intrusive worries and thoughts, nightmares, and excessive worrying are all symptoms of vicarious trauma. Just as we want first responders to reach out for help, we also want impacted loved ones to get help. Do not be afraid to seek services and please understand that what you are experiencing is valid. It is important to get help yourself so you can get back to your baseline level of functioning as quickly as possible.

Code Four: Surviving and Thriving in Public Safety

Justin's Story

For the first time in eleven years, I have been able to clearly process experiences from Iraq without completely breaking down. I served in the United States Army for five years and take pride in calling myself a combat veteran. I am currently a police officer and have been on the force for almost ten years, working in various undercover assignments.

Time to Grow Up:
As a child, I was fascinated by war and grew up watching war movies. I remember telling my parents that I wanted to go to war like my grandpa and uncle (WWII/Vietnam combat vets). I now fully understand the phrase, "Be careful what you wish for." I joined the United States Army at the age of nineteen. I found that I needed a change in life because the road I was going down, well, I would most likely end up in prison or worse. I needed something that would change me as a person. However, I never really knew how this would completely turn my world upside down. After a year of college, and realizing that my life was quickly going nowhere, I enlisted in the United States Army Reserve as a weapons specialist. When I returned back home, I found myself in the same rut and going down the same road that I had been on before. After a lot of convincing my chain of command, I was discharged from the Reserves and enlisted full time in the United States Army,

with an MOS (military occupational specialty) change as a Cavalry Scout.

Off to war:
Well, I definitely got what I wanted as a child!

In the fall of 2006, my unit was deployed to Mosul, Iraq. We would not see home until the last month of 2007. As most of you know, this was the most violent time of the Iraqi War and a lot of American lives were lost, including my mentor, Sergeant Wilson, and my fellow scouts, Corporal Hernandez and Corporal Hilbert.

During the next fifteen months, I guess you can say we were basically in the shit from the time we unpacked until the time we packed and locked that fucking Conex box for the last time. From doing SKTs (Sniper Killer Teams) and HKTs (Hunter Killer Teams) to IEDs (Improvised Explosive Devices), being ambushed and mortared, and finding a bunch of dudes who'd been beheaded, it was one hell of a deployment, to say the least.

So, let's get to it...

Some of the things that keep me up at night:
I remember my truck being hit by an IED for the first time. We were on a patrol through Mosul, and I was gunning the truck. As we were driving down the road, I remember seeing a small child standing off to the side of the road watching as our convoy of armored Humvees drove past him. I remember as we came closer to passing the child, I rotated the turret and observed a male laying

down on his stomach in an elevated walkway that looked over us. As soon as it clicked in my mind that we were about to get ambushed or blown up, my truck was hit by an IED. As we continued to push through the blast, I remember feeling a warm spray covering my body, followed by heat and a mouthful of warm liquid. As I came to, I realized that I was covered by whatever remained of this child and the liquid that was in my mouth was this child's blood. I remember my crazy-ass driver, who looked up at me and began laughing at me, asking me if I had just seen what happened. Maybe I was in shock, but I also started to laugh as we pushed through, and began to rinse myself off with water.

When I was over there, I remember doing one of the "Hearts and Minds"-type missions, where we went to a school and dropped off school supplies and played with Iraqi children in an attempt to show that we wanted to do good for their country. Sometime after we left and before we went back out there the next day, the fucking cowards (insurgents) decided that they would take over the school and place large amounts of explosives inside the school while the children were still inside. Their master plan was to detonate the explosives once we were inside the school. Well, that did not happen and they blew up the entire school, with the children inside it, before we were able to arrive at the school. I remember us driving to the school when they blew it up. I remember thinking to myself, "Fuck, they wouldn't have done that with all those kids in there, would they?" I remember pulling up to the school and smelling burnt flesh and hearing people screaming. It was complete fucking chaos; it looked like a scene from a horror movie. I just remember thinking to myself, "Why? Come kill me instead of the kids. Fight me, you fucking cowards."

September 7, 2007 was my worst day in Iraq. Typing this out now still fucks with my head and trying to articulate this is extremely hard because, besides my own personal shit, I watched some of the best leaders I know to this day fall apart. This day was when I lost three brothers. When I first arrived at my duty station, Sergeant Wilson was my team leader. He was my mentor. He taught me everything there is to know about the Army, leadership, being a scout, reconnaissance, and even helped me get promoted to sergeant. He was that type of team leader you could call day or night; if you were in a pinch or needed something, he was there. I loved him like a brother and had the utmost respect for him.

During my deployment, we moved out of Mosul proper and went to Badush and to Tal Afar. Part of our mission was to set up a base near Badush Prison due to it constantly being attacked. I remember us stopping at Badush Prison after coming off a long operation. I remember being dead tired and was finally able to get some sleep. I remember lifting my head up and making eye contact with Sergeant Wilson and us both acknowledging each other. I could see that he looked extremely drained and knowing that he had been more than likely out doing an SKT (Sniper Killer Team) the night before.

After we acknowledged each other, I fell asleep. When I woke up, we left and I remember I could not find Sergeant Wilson prior to leaving. We went out, did another op, and returned to our base in Tal Afar. I remember that night we had plans to go back out to the prison to do more reconnaissance ops, since insurgency was extremely high at this place.

I remember being awakened in the middle of the night and told to go to HQ. Being half asleep and not realizing what was going on, we had a formation and I remember my Commander and First Sergeant exit the tent. I remember seeing these men have actual emotion on their faces for the first time. They then broke the news that members of 2nd platoon were in a firefight during the night and that we lost three men. I remember my stomach dropping and feeling sick. Then they told us the names of our fallen: Sergeant Wilson, Corporal Hernandez, Corporal Hilbert. I remember one of the best leaders of my platoon falling out of formation and walking away. I remember feeling angry, but having no emotion whatsoever. Once we were excused from formation, I remember walking back to my bunk and wondering why I wasn't crying. My fucking mentor had just died during his third or fourth combat tour and I didn't feel anything. What the fuck was wrong with me?

The next day we drove out to the Badush Prison. I remember the entire trip like it was yesterday. Silence. No one spoke on the radio, no one spoke to each other on the truck. Everyone was extremely focused on one thing. We were all looking for an excuse to kill an Iraqi while driving there. We were all angry. When we arrived at the prison, I remember talking to some of my brothers in 2nd platoon. I remember them saying that they had killed a bunch of those fuckers that night, but jokingly said not enough of them and that they were pissed off because they could not find one of our brother's arm or leg (I forget which one).

The rest of my tour was filled with more violence, more IEDs, more firefights, the cowards using children as human shields. More booms, more bangs. It was one giant shit show. I remember that so many guys were dying in Mosul that it felt like months would go by where we could not make phone calls or email family and friends at home because of the death notices being made back home.

I made it out alive. Now what?
Coming home, I remember going through all the "Don't hit your spouse" classes and then sent on leave. Coming home was probably one of the hardest things for me. I was not ready to be home, and I don't think my friends and family were ready for me. My entire outlook on life had changed and, at the time, I did not have respect for people who wanted to voice their opinion on how this country was being run when they truly had no idea what the rest of the world was like. Come to think of it, I still have an issue with that. I remember coming back from a

local bar with some of my high school friends, where the entire time I stood in a corner by myself looking at everyone who walked into the bar. I remember not being able to hold a conversation with any of my "normal" friends because at the time I did not know how to act with them. I did not know how to present myself to "normal" people or hold a "normal" conversation. I remember one of my friends dropping me at my mom's house after the bar. I ran into the house and went straight to my room and closed the door and began to break down crying. I didn't know what I was doing. I remember my mother coming into my room and asking me what was wrong. I remember telling her that I didn't have anything in common with my friends anymore. I remember trying to explain to her that I had never been more confused in my life on how I should act. For the first time in my life, I felt alone and disconnected from the world that I once knew and loved.

I remember getting married to my wife of almost eleven years now—we jokingly call our first three years of marriage the "Dark Days." When we were first married, I was fucking horrible. I remember her trying to wake me up while I was screaming and crying in my sleep. I would wake up and begin yelling and screaming at nothing, punching holes through the walls of our first apartment. I remember being angry all the time and wanting to go back to Iraq because that's what I knew. I knew how to live there, I knew how to act there, I felt normal there. I also remember urinating the bed a lot due to the night terrors that I was having. I felt completely embarrassed about the situation. I mean, here I am, a grown-ass man, not even drunk, and pissing the bed over a bad dream. I would just leave and drive off in the middle of the night and return in the morning, so confused and lost. I remember my wife laying on the floor with me at 3 a.m. when she found me blackout drunk, crying, and saying that I should have died over there, not my friends. I miss my friends. I never got to say goodbye. It should have been me who died. I'm ready to die, I want to die. She even told me that I said I wanted to kill myself, which to this day I don't ever remember saying because I was too drunk and such an emotional drunk mess that I would wake up a day and a half later trying to figure out what I had done or said. I don't know why she stayed with me through all of this but, if I can just say one thing about her, it's that she's been my rock through everything. I can honestly say that if it wasn't for her, I probably wouldn't be here today.

Realizing I needed help:
Through the course of all of this, I got married, had two beautiful girls, and became a police officer. In 2018 my wife and I decided to make health goals for us. You know that "New Year, New Me" hipster shit. My goals consisted of going to the doctor for a checkup, starting the VA process, losing weight, and the very last thing was trying to see someone for PTSD.

    Through the course of time I gained a lot of

weight, and my mental state was only being fixed by a bottle of whiskey. I found myself drinking more and more, like a handle of whiskey in two days along with a case of beer. I remember looking at myself in a mirror and being disgusted by what I saw. I remember saying, "Wow, what the fuck have I done to myself? Is this how you want your girls to remember you?"

In September 2018, I was having one of "those weeks." I remember sitting on the couch and telling myself, "I can't do this anymore, I am exhausted from feeling this way, my family is exhausted from me feeling this way. I am ready. I am ready to get actual help." I began researching for a place that specialized in treating veterans and found Tania Glenn & Associates. To be honest, I was very skeptical. I have read a lot of horror stories about guys being heavily medicated and the therapy not working for them, and guys coming out of a therapy session feeling like they were being judged because of the things they had to do over there. I did not want that. I emailed Tania and asked her some questions and for some more information about the type of therapy she provided.

Getting help:
To think of this now, I can't believe I put myself and my family through this for over eleven years. The first meeting I had with Tania, I was skeptical and didn't really know what to expect. The office setting was extremely private and comfortable. We began talking about my

experience of being in Iraq and the issues I had from the aftermath of it all. Tania explained to me that I would be a great candidate for Eye Movement Desensitization and Reprocessing (EMDR). Tania explained to me the entire process and advised me to take days off after each treatment.

I did a total of two sessions of EMDR and I must say, it kicked my ass. The aftermath of each session was extremely hard, as well. I was definitely out of commission for a few days after the first session and over a week after the second. I had a constant migraine and the constant ringing that I had in my ears increased. I felt like I did when I first returned from Iraq. As the fog lifted, however, I began to realize how much my triggers had diminished. I completely stopped having night terrors. Life was different. Life was better.

It's almost January and I can honestly say I feel good. I know that my issues will never go away, the memories of the things I did and saw are mine forever. I haven't had any "episodes" since my last treatment in December.

In closing:
To all the veterans and law enforcement out there who are on the fence about getting help, I hope you read this and it pushes you to get the help you need. We, as a community, we have done so much, have been through so much, and have given so much that at the very least we should be able to enjoy our lives and live in peace.

Code Four: Surviving and Thriving in Public Safety

A flight nurse back in the helicopter after an incident

Chapter Six

Large-Scale Events and Disasters

Now the dark begins to rise
Save your breath, it's far from over
Leave the lost and dead behind
Now's your chance to run for cover

"I Will Now Bow" by Breaking Benjamin

Caring for first responders during and after large-scale incidents is a vital piece of every deployment. We cannot expect our first responders to deploy or respond to the unimaginable and return to normal operations without a good plan in place to assure this really happens. Being invited to a disaster is an honor and a privilege. It has been some of the most rewarding work in my career.

Control the Chaos

The nature of disasters creates some problems in terms of scene control and the quality of care. In almost every large-scale event I have been asked to deploy to, there

Code Four: Surviving and Thriving in Public Safety

are clinicians and peer support or critical incident teams that will just show up to help. This only adds to the chaos and creates confusion, frustration, and causes more problems than help. I strongly discourage self-deployment when I do peer support training, and I prohibit it on teams I manage. I encourage all leaders and incident commanders to promptly remove anyone who shows up uninvited.

After 9/11, I remember seeing therapists who showed up on the outskirts of Ground Zero. Every day, as the first responders were ending their shifts consisting of the gruesome task of digging and finding bodies, these self-deployed therapists would be outside waiting for them. As most Americans were waving flags, cheering the first responders on and thanking them for what they do, the therapists were grabbing their arms and asking them if they needed to be debriefed. You can imagine the responses of the very seasoned, hardened, yet exhausted firefighters and police officers! Personally, it made me sick to see this.

Any team invited to a disaster or large-scale event should remember: this call is a privilege. This is not your glorious victory or some self-aggrandizing moment. This means it is time to go to work, to give it your very best, and stay focused and humble.

Incident command or the leadership in charge of recruiting Peer Support Teams should provide a list and issue very clear instructions to their teams. The list should consist of what to bring, what to wear, what to pack, and what to leave at home. The instructions must be clear and detailed. The moment teams begin to deviate from the list or the instructions will be the moment those teams need to be sent home.

Disaster Mental Health

Prior to deploying, I encourage all departments and agencies to plan and schedule an after-deployment education brief for everyone who goes to the disaster or major event. This should be considered a portion of the deployment and should be a paid event. First responders should commit to the educational brief before deploying.

Once deployed, it is imperative that first responders pace themselves and maintain a consistent and cautious work/sleep schedule. It is very hard to pace yourself when the call to help others and save lives is overwhelming. First responders will work until they drop, which is, of course, dangerous. Not pacing rescuers will cause them to fatigue and be out of commission. It is far more advantageous to mandate down time.

It is also important to keep fingers on the emotional pulse of how first responders are doing. I strongly encourage appropriate interventions, at the right moment, to enhance first responder resilience.

The **first intervention** is scene support. I train my Peer Support Teams to do this very important intervention. Armed with water, snacks, sport drinks, gloves, supplies, and anything first responders might need, my

Code Four: Surviving and Thriving in Public Safety

teams will "work the crowd" as first responders are taking a break. In doing so, they are not only assisting with the physical needs of the first responders, they are also placing their fingers on their mental pulse to determine how they are doing.

Peer Support Team members doing scene support will check in with their first responders to see whether or not they have had a chance to call home, how the rest of their team is doing, if they have had enough hydration and nutrition to last them for a while, and to assert what their job assignment is for the remainder of the shift.

As simple as it may sound, it is nonetheless very important work. Peer Support Team members are assuring that psychological resilience is being maintained and making sure that responders are not overwhelmed.

The **second intervention** is the educational brief. At the end of the disaster's first day, each person on scene should receive literature reiterating normal reactions to stress and stress management strategies. It is a form of inoculation, because once first responders understand that they are normal and once they know what to do about stress, it will build their resilience. I always refer to the literature as "refrigerator material" and ask first responders to take it home and put it on their refrigerator for their loved ones to read.

Throughout the remainder of the disaster, Peer Support Teams remain available for one-on-one additional advice and education and any form of support needed. They should also be active in post-deployment briefs. The entire process is designed to promote resilience and assure the mental wellness of everyone on scene.

First Responders in Disasters

Large-scale disasters demand significant physical and mental energy, which public servants readily give of themselves. However, the recovery process for these amazing first responders is frequently overlooked.

First responders take about half a second to ramp up mentally and physically. The fight-or-flight response is immediate and vital to the roles that first responders take on during dangerous and even life-threatening situations. Coming off the response, however, is very different. Think of this analogy: launching into response mode is fast like a microwave, with immediate heat and energy. Coming off response mode is like an oven that has been cooking at 500 degrees cooling down, slowly and gradually.

During disasters, all first responders utilize the fight-or-flight response, which involves the sympathetic nervous system and copious amounts of adrenaline, glucose, and cortisol. In the aftermath of the activation, rescuers will experience the counter effect of the fight-or-flight response, which is a parasympathetic nervous system backlash. This means rescuers hit the wall. They get very tired and irritable. They sometimes catch colds or don't feel well. At the same time, they also begin to deal

Code Four: Surviving and Thriving in Public Safety

with reality as the sights, smells, and sounds begin to replay in their minds.

I ask first responders to give themselves time to re-adjust and to understand they are not light switches. They do not simply flip on disaster mode, only to flip it off again when they get home. Readjusting back to home and work is a process that takes time and patience. Here are the recommendations I give to first responders when they return home:

- Get rest. Take plenty of naps if you are not sleeping well through the night.
- Stay hydrated.
- Take vitamin C and zinc to help prevent or shorten the nasty cold you might have.
- Talk to your family, your peers, peer support, or a clinician.
- Resist the urge to skip the gym. Yes, you are tired, but moving your body is the best way to get the fight-or-flight chemicals out of your system.
- Resist the urge to drink too much. Heavy intoxication will only make matters worse.
- If after two weeks you feel like you are not beginning to return to normal, get help immediately from a clinician who understands public safety.

First Responder Families and Disasters

As first responders are deployed, it can be very challenging to be a family member left behind. Not receiving updates is one of the hardest and most frustrating things to go through when your loved one is deployed. First responders returning from deployment can be very difficult for families to manage. Their loved ones may be ramped up, disengaged, distant, irritated, or bark orders without cause. All of this indicates they are still very much in the adjustment period and communication about this phase is essential. If both the first responder and their family members are aware this is going on, the next step is to communicate as well as possible to help the first responder get through the adjustment period.

The following are recommendations I give to family members:

- It is important to give first responders time and space to return to "normal life." Try not to overwhelm them with requests in the first few days. They will need time to restore their resilience.
- If there are issues at home while your loved one is away and you are notifying them, be sure to include the solutions that are being implemented. For example, if your tenth grader is struggling in biology, let your loved one know what steps are being taken for tutoring, etc.

- Understand that your first responder has seen significant human struggling. They will come home with a perspective that little things in life don't REALLY matter. It is likely that they will have little tolerance when their kids argue over what video game to play. They are still dealing with the sharp contrast of the reality from where they have been.
- Don't be surprised if your first responder has no desire to go out in public for a few days. They have been over-stimulated by noise, people, and chaos.
- Understand that your loved one might not want to talk about it. It's okay for little snippets to come out here and there, and also for them to be more inclined to share with their fellow first responders versus family members.
- Don't take it personally if your loved one tells you that they want to go back. This is normal. The work is very meaningful. Much help is needed and ongoing in disasters. It is normal to want to return to continue to help.

Colleagues and Buddies

For coworkers and friends, it is tempting to ask first responders to tell you all about it. Initially this is a daunting question, because it is hard to conceptualize where to begin. "Tell us all about it" was said to me after both the

Oklahoma City Bombing and my first trip to New York after 9/11. In 1995, when I returned from Oklahoma City, I simply did not know how to answer the question, so I shut down completely for a few weeks. In the aftermath of 9/11, I talked a lot about how amazing the Peer Support Program was at the NYPD. I chose this route because it was safe to talk about NYPD and avoid any triggers. Definitely a good lesson learned from two tough deployments.

The following is what I recommend for coworkers:
- Be there for your colleagues as they return and allow them the opportunity to discuss what they have been through without judgment.
- Understand that they will view the normal workday as mundane for a while. Considering what they have been through, it is normal for returning first responders to be frustrated with the tempo, the paperwork, and the protocol. They will feel restricted compared to where they have been.
- Encourage them to get help if things are not returning to normal.

Staying Grounded

One of the most important things I have learned about disaster deployments is the importance of staying grounded. In a disaster, staying grounded means keeping tabs on and in touch with the rest of life, and maintaining a steady stream of consciousness that life is going on outside of the disaster.

When deployed to a disaster, it is very easy for the event to take over. It feels as though nothing else matters and the only focus is the event and what is in front of you. It is a very dangerous mindset, because no disaster lasts forever, no deployment lasts forever, and if you are not ready to return home when it is time, it is going to be a very bumpy transition. As a matter of fact, if first responders do not stay grounded, they will feel as though they have been ripped right out of the disaster scene and thrown back into their houses. This never goes well.

The key to staying grounded is to call home every day and to speak to your family. It is important to check and respond to emails, voicemails, and other forms of communication. It is a reminder that life is going on without you, and that you will return to normal life at some point.

Another way to stay grounded is to mentally prepare yourself to go home. When I am deployed, I wake up each morning and have a conversation in my head. I tell myself what day it is in relation to what day we are going home. I think about my obligations on the day I return, the day after I return, and so on. I remind myself that this deployment is temporary and, although I will be tired when I get home, my family will be super energized to see me and I need to be ready. I remind myself of the sacrifices they make when I am gone and how important it is to make it up to them.

When I deployed with a Peer Support Team to the Oklahoma City bombing, disaster mental health was really an unknown. We worked sixteen-hour days and had some very tough assignments. We rarely had the chance to call home and none of us really knew of its importance. We slid into our final day with no preparation to return home and no decompression period. We were numb, and we were all struggling with how to go back to our normal lives.

As we arrived home on a Thursday night, I really didn't know what to do with myself other than return to my shift on Friday night in the emergency room where I worked at the time. I walked into the ER on that Friday night with three long shifts ahead. As I walked down the hallway, I realized that I felt as though I had been gone for an eternity, and everything felt different. I felt "off." I began to wonder why this was happening. I soon figured it out. I had not stayed grounded.

My first referral that night was a nineteen-year-old female, in for an amoxicillin overdose. That's right, she took ten amoxicillin in an "overdose" attempt because she was upset at her boyfriend for giving another girl attention.

At that point, my main memory is me yelling at the referring ER physician that this was "bullshit" and that I was not going to see her. I also remembered saying something along the lines of "I will show you what a real crisis looks like." Fortunately, this physician was one of the more laid-back doctors, and he simply looked at me and asked if I was ready to be back. My defensive "of course I am" was total nonsense, but somehow, I got through the shift and the subsequent shifts without getting in trouble, but I really was not okay. It wasn't until I had the chance to process what happened in Oklahoma City that I was truly okay. The biggest mistake was not staying grounded and not preparing to return home.

During some disasters, teams are able to build in an extra day for decompression. As much as everyone wants to go home, this is a great way to give your brain time to begin the adjustment process. Each time we went to New York after 9/11, we would leave Manhattan on Friday afternoon and go to Long Island, where we would stay for the night and fly home on Saturday morning. We used this time as a team to bring our energy down a few notches. We would go see a movie, go to dinner, call home, and out-brief with each other as a team. Most importantly, after six days with the amazing NYPD, we would make a swear jar and deposit a dollar every time we threw an "F bomb." It was a great way to clean up our language before going home. Typically, I would deposit $20 at a time because it was just easier than depositing money each time. Later, we donated the money to The Red Cross.

Burnout Resulting from Disasters

During large-scale events and disasters, first responders

who are a little, somewhat, or very burned out often experience significantly more complicated burnout at the end of a disaster.

Burnout is the result of coupling extremely high, sometimes unrealistic expectations with good intentions, and not having enough balance in one's life.

The onset of burnout happens slowly. The process is hard to identify, because it can be quite subtle. As I stated in Chapter One, by the time this is happening, first responders are definitely in the End of the Innocence phase. They are somewhat jaded and scarred.

Then we ask those first responders to go to a disaster and give 150% of themselves, possibly more than once. While deployed, burnout sits on the back burner because the mission is important and meaningful. At this point, I warn first responders to not get sucked into the notion that your burnout is no longer there because you are feeling great about the present mission. Instead, be prepared for your burnout to be exacerbated upon your return home. Be prepared so you can tackle it.

Getting through burnout involves restoring your resilience. It's not hard, and small changes pay off big time. The process requires looking at your life and figuring out how to regain the balance between work and your personal time, between negative stress and positive stress. Begin by focusing on the basics: health, hydration, nutrition, rest, exercise. Then tackle the more advanced concepts: your family, friends, hobbies, faith. Focus on the things that make you who you are outside

Code Four: Surviving and Thriving in Public Safety

of the job. These are the things you will have in your life when you retire. Foster these aspects of your life. You may even have to teach yourself how to have fun again.

Recovering from burnout sometimes means modifying the amount of time you work. Changing your role or duties (if possible), picking up healthy habits like exercise, letting go of unhealthy habits like excessive alcohol consumption, finding new hobbies, making new friends, and reconnecting with your loved ones. Once you have conquered burnout, your life, energy, sense of humor, and outlook will be monumentally better than they once were.

In my practice, I have found that employees who have recovered from burnout often become some of the best assets to their departments. They carry an infinite amount of wisdom and personal experience with them, and they tend to look out for others who may be headed down the same path. The most qualified person to recognize a fellow employee's burnout is another first responder who has already been there.

On a final note, it is important to mention that burnout often mimics major depression. If you choose to talk to someone in my line of work, be sure to find a clinician who understands the public safety culture and who is very sensitive to the differences between burnout and clinical depression. Being labeled by someone with good intentions but limited experience with first responders will simply generate more problems than solutions.

Chapter Seven
Special Operations

Comin' for you, we're the cowboys from hell
Step aside, we're the cowboys from hell

"Cowboys from Hell" by Pantera

Special operations—SWAT, tactical medics, rescue, airborne law enforcement, air medical, and special operations groups—are all unique cultures within the culture of public safety. Special operations personnel are all highly driven and dedicated. They are mentally and physically fit. First responders in special operations have navigated their careers successfully and have challenged themselves to reach the highest level of skill, strength, and ability.

Because of the nature of special operations missions, first responders in these roles are likely to be exposed to higher levels of stress, trauma, and chaos. Special operations teams are not utilized when everything is fine. Rather, they are launched when events are dangerous, out of control, and traumatic.

Resiliency in first responders in special operations is a given. They have demonstrated mental and physical strength, skills, knowledge, and the ability to stay calm and think under intense pressure. Special operators in public safety frequently view themselves as immune to stress. No one is completely immune to stress. Given the right circumstances, anyone can be impacted negatively and suffer as a result. The challenge: to help these teams understand that due to the nature of their work, they must have a solid plan of action in place to restore their mental health.

Hearts and Minds

One of the most interesting project experiences of my career has been my work with the United States Border Patrol. Contracted to care for the SOG (Special Operations Group) of the Border Patrol, I had to familiarize myself quickly with their line of work. While their missions are sometimes different, the two teams that make up the Border Patrol SOG work in conjunction and perform amazing and difficult work. They are dedicated, strong, cohesive, and very driven. They are also very closed off. I knew they were not going to simply trust me, and that I would have to earn their respect. I began by completing training in each sector across the country. I traveled west to east, providing education on trauma and resilience. My first stop was San Diego in July. I rode with them on their marine patrol. An unexpected highlight was the appearance of playful dolphins racing along our vessel and a visit with seals sunning on rocks. I absorbed as much of the Border Patrol's culture and terminology in the time spent to become proficient in understanding and speaking their Border Patrol language.

My second trip was quite different. Traveling west to east, I went to Yuma, AZ, at 118 degrees during the day in August. It was a "dry heat," they said. One of the agents I was riding along with looked at me one day and asked if I had my passport on me. I did not. He mentioned that he would have to leave me in Mexico since "that was where we were at the moment." The sheer panic on my face caused him to laugh for hours. I did, too, once I made extra sure he was joking. It was his way to impress on me the uncertainty of the territory.

My third stop was Tucson Sector, where the serious work really began. A second trip had been scheduled in advance due to the enormity of the sector. This was about a year and a half after Special Agent Brian Terry was killed near Rio Rico, in far southern Arizona. Agent Terry's death was traumatic, controversial, and at that point unsolved.

As I walked into Tucson Sector and began my first brief, the first thing I noticed was the palpable level of agents' anger and pain. I immediately noticed thousand-yard stares and blank expressions. As I finished the first brief, three things happened. First, many agents approached and asked to speak with me, either right then or in private later. The second thing that occurred was that the agents attending the first brief told the rest of the team that the brief was "10-8," which is Border Patrol speak for good to go. The third occurrence happened when the commander took me aside, called headquarters, and asked that I return to Tucson for a total of five trips, promptly authorized.

When requests for help like this occur, I make it a point not get overwhelmed and to take things as though I am running a marathon—one mile at a time. The first step was the education brief, which is outlined in *First Responder Resilience: Caring for Public Servants*. The agents responded so overwhelmingly to the education on the chemistry of the fight-or-flight reaction, and on the four types of stress and resilience building, that they began to approach me with increasing questions.

The next step was to learn and understand the event involving Special Agent Terry and what occurred afterwards. I soon realized that the Tucson Sector Peer Support Team had done a phenomenal job, but that local clinicians had failed the special operations. During one of the initial briefs, I learned that a mental health professional had referred to one of the teams by the wrong designation. Despite the fact that they corrected him, he continued to use the wrong term, which of course had the result of shutting down the team's trust. I also learned that no one had received EMDR or any sort of evidence-based trauma care after an event.

Knowing that special operation groups (SOGs) are

very guarded, my third intervention was to spend time with them in the field, away from the sector. My first ride-along could not have gone better. As we headed out, radio traffic picked up and some agents indicated they were tracking a group. As we headed that way, I assured the agent I was with that I could run fast and not to worry about me in a foot pursuit. He told me his instructions were to make sure I did not get hurt, and we were good to go.

Our foot pursuit lasted several minutes and went through low brush. We did not end up catching the group of illegals that day, but we did find their dope—four hundred pounds, to be exact. As we came to a stop, I noticed all kinds of small lacerations with blood dripping down my arms. As the agents turned around to see if I was still behind them, I made the comment, "I realize now why you all wear long sleeves even when it's hot as hell." Their looks were priceless. One agent said, "We've only had her for two hours and Dr. Glenn is already torn up." I realized they were a little freaked out, so I replied, "Are you kidding? This is the BEST day ever! And call me Tania." They laughed and indicated that perhaps I was just as crazy as the rest of them.

This ride-along was a pivotal point to the success of accomplishing the fourth intervention, which is the trauma work and healing I needed to do. Rapport and trust were no longer an issue. Now agents began to ask for help. Whether it was as involved as EMDR or an informal "bullshit session" in the parking lot (which is never bullshit but actually very serious), the healing began. It was hard work and one of the most rewarding experiences of my career.

Having a Plan for SOG

The importance of caring for the hearts and minds of special operations groups is not always as simple as using the departmental plan. First responders in special operations often want their own plan that they can trust.

I highly recommend that some of the SOG team members go through peer support training to assist their teams. If a traumatic event involves peer support members, the ability to reach out to other SOG Peer Support Teams from different departments is very helpful. The presence of a well-trained Peer Support Team that understands the culture, the terminology, and the mission will absolutely mitigate the healing process.

I also recommend that special operations groups find the right clinicians to assist. Recruiting and spending time with them is paramount. Taking them to the field or inviting them to training will help them understand the nature of their work. This is labor-intensive and a long process, but it is worth it. When a team finds someone they trust, they will use them to restore their resilience and keep them mentally fit. The whole point is for first responders in special operations to begin to care for their minds as well as they care for their bodies.

After an air medical crash several years ago, I

spent time with the local EAP counselors who wanted me to help them with their ability to connect with and help air crews. After training on trauma and PTSD, I encouraged them to visit the stations, spend time with the crews, and to go on some flights. When I mentioned going on flights, the entire room looked at me as if I was crazy. I asked them to explain their reaction, and one clinician said, "Well, they crashed." I pointed out that here lies the problem—flying is good enough for the nurses and paramedics, but not for them? I also pointed out that this company takes thousands of flights per year with only one crash in their history. While not a pleasant event, it is statistically far safer than driving to and from their offices every day. They heard me, the point was made, but they did not change their minds. My final comment to them: their refusal to truly understand what it's like to serve in an air medical capacity, yet the desire for air medical crews to come see them for therapy, did not do anyone any good. I found this very frustrating.

Annual Resilience Assessments with Clinicians

Many of my customers facilitate annual resilience assessments. We go onsite and visit each member of the department. This is a time to speak to us, totally off the record, to address current resilience, goals, and areas for life improvement. My team is able to help first responders set goals and objectives to reach those goals, as well as identify possible resources. I absolutely believe this should be a norm for special operations groups.

The ability to check in, address how things are going, and problem-solve on life challenges is extremely helpful. It gives operators a chance to evaluate their lives, strengthen certain areas, and work on improving their overall health.

Special Considerations for Loved Ones

Being in a relationship with a special operations first responder has its inherent challenges. Being in a relationship with an SOG first responder can be even more challenging. The key is to embrace the role as much as possible and adapt to it as well as you can. It is difficult to make plans with someone who is on call. When callouts happen, everything gets dropped suddenly, and you are left holding down the fort—home and life—for up to several days at a time. This can be frustrating, and it can very easily feel as though the job always comes first and you are a distant second.

The key is to communicate throughout. It is important to balance work and personal life, so the down times, the times when your first responder is not on call or even the planned time off is the time to really reconnect. It is sometimes helpful to talk to other loved ones and ask how they cope with their first responders. Most loved ones are able to adapt to the demands of special operations over time simply by getting used to the tempo and allowing adjustment periods.

Bob's Story

Colors and a Shape

A deep blue, so deep that it appears almost purple and a pale trapezoid with blurred edges.

That one color that is so unique and specific and that one pale shape, so blurred that it almost isn't real. Two things that seem so innocuous, but those two little things almost destroyed me.

Colors and a shape.

I'm a career paramedic, and I consider myself to be quite experienced, which is just a professional way to say that I've done a lot and seen more than just a thing or two. I've got more than twenty years of experience under my belt, working in several states. I currently work in a very busy urban EMS system, and I specialize in rescue. I've deployed as a rescue worker for dozens of natural disasters across the United States. Early in my career, I worked for the coroner's office of a very populated county; my job was to pick up bodies from crime scenes and accidents and transport them to autopsy. So yeah, I've been around the proverbial block, and I'm no stranger to death.

A few years ago, I was dealing with some stressful operational shit at work. Nothing big, as it turned out, but stressful nonetheless. While that was going on, I found myself assigned as a rescue medic to a law enforcement dive team working a body recovery, providing team medical support and ultimately pronouncing the victim. There wasn't anything remarkable about the assignment until they found the teenager's body, a victim of suicide, and brought it to me. He had drowned in cold water in the middle of winter, and when an officer opened the body bag, I was confronted by a boy whose face was frozen in a gasp of horror and whose skin was a deep blue, so deep that it appeared almost purple. I did my job, and when I started the paperwork, I found out that this young man had the same name as my infant son. I accompanied the body back to the dock on the boat with officer, and when we tied up, I said goodbye and walked away. But for some reason I couldn't forget his face... or the color of his skin.

Three days later, back on shift again, I was dispatched to a water rescue that turned into a drowning. A young father who couldn't swim well had gone into the water in a pool under a waterfall in hopes of rescuing his dog, who was having difficulty swimming. I arrived on scene in my dry suit, ready to work, and was immediately sent into the water. I spent fifty-two minutes in the water before we pulled him out. He was about ten feet deep and floating face down. He was wearing dark shorts, had dark hair, and his arms and head were hanging down as he floated. The water was so murky that as I dove down to him all I could see was the pale, lighter color of his back, forming kind of a blurry trapezoid from his belt to his shoulders. With the help of my partner and several firefighters, we were able to pull him to the surface and swim him to shore. When we got him there, my partner and I were so fatigued that we couldn't walk. We handed him to a fresh pair of medics and group of firefighters, and we crawled out of the water, then collapsed onto the rocky shore. We cleared that call, got cleaned up, and ran calls for the rest of our shift, but I couldn't get the image of the shape of his back out of my mind, that pale trapezoid with blurred edges.

Over the next few weeks, weird stuff started to happen to me. I began to have nightmares, but I couldn't remember what they were about. Then I began having nightmares about my deployment and work during and after Hurricane Katrina, an event that was almost ten years in my past. Then I began to remember having dreams of a deep, almost purplish-blue colored face, frozen in a silent scream, and a pale trapezoid with blurred edges. I started waking up in the night covered in sweat and panicked, so I started to have a stiff drink or so before going to bed. I began to see the blue-purple shape and that pale trapezoid in flashes while I was awake. I drank more. Months went by. One night during my shift, I was lying in bed in the dark, at work, in my uniform fleece pullover. I was hot, so I began to pull it off while still lying down. Somehow that dammed fleece got tangled around my head and arms while I tried to pull it off. Simple to fix, but for some reason my brain told me that I was in the water and that I was drowning. I started to panic. I don't know how I got out of that stupid fleece, but I remember pacing the bedroom telling myself to calm the fuck down. "You're a rescue medic, you're a swift-water rescue specialist, water is nothing to you, calm the fuck down!" I repeated this to myself over and over again. I had a drink that morning when I got home from work. I was getting worse, and I didn't know why. I realized that I was getting sullen and moody with my family, and I was snapping at little things. I was dreading going to work. I was drinking about a liter of hard liquor a week and I don't know how much wine. I was falling apart.

At work one day I was scrolling through my email. I saw an email that was a few weeks old about a "mental health for first responders" class that Tania Glenn was putting on for whoever was interested in my department. That stuck in my head too. The next morning at home I told my wife about the class and said, "I think I should go to this." She agreed, and the next day I was in a classroom with a small handful of my coworkers listening to Tania talk about mental stress, adrenal insufficiency, cortisol level problems, and a whole bevy of signs and symptoms of PTSD. As Tania went down that list of PTSD symptoms, I was saying to myself "check, check, check, check..." It was then that I realized just how much trouble I was in.

I spent the rest of the class preparing to approach Tania. I composed a whole little speech and everything. I waited for the classroom to clear some and when Tania was free, I approached her. I approached the woman whom I had known casually for over fifteen years and I took one look at her, opened my mouth to recite my speech, and couldn't. What I did instead was start crying and gasped, "I need help." And Tania, the woman who had known me and had been at least somewhat aware of my career for fifteen years, instantly knew how hurt I was. She was able to get me talking, and I unloaded everything about the drownings, the colors and the shapes, right there standing in the classroom. Tania had me in her office the next morning.

We spoke more in depth about everything and Tania suggested that we try EMDR. I agreed, and we set a date not too far in the future for me to return. Tania wove her magic and it worked. The session was easy and short. I was dubious, but as I walked out of Tania's office, I actually felt better—tired, but better. That day I collapsed in a nap on my couch and didn't have a nightmare. That night I didn't drink and I slept through the night, again with no nightmares.

It's been several years since my experience with PTSD and EMDR. The bottom line is, EMDR worked. I'm still at work, and maybe still alive, because of Tania and her practice. I've gotten to the point that I can discuss my experience with others without having problems. Okay, when I talk about the colors and shape, my jaw clenches and I begin to sweat, but that's minor and easy to deal with compared to how it was.

For those of us in public safety, death and mayhem are just another day at work, and we grow used to it. We think it doesn't affect us, but it does. We think about,

Code Four: Surviving and Thriving in Public Safety

and maybe even prepare for, being hurt or dying in an MVA, or an active shooter, on the scene of a domestic violence call, or a fire. We think about the big calls, but it's the little things that can end us... perhaps more than the big things. For me, it was colors and a shape.

I'm a paramedic, my business is saving lives. Tania Glenn saved mine.

The location where Brian Terry was killed

The dope we caught during my ridealong

Chapter Eight

Retirement

The sun begins to rise and wash away the sky
The turning of the tide, don't leave it all behind
And I will never say goodbye

"Angels Fall" by Breaking Benjamin

There is a saying: *What do cops do when they retire? They die.* I hate this saying. I hate it because many times it is true, and I just can't stand it. After all your years of service to others, countless incidents involving blood, sweat, and tears, you are supposed to retire, finally live normally and be happy. But somehow this does not happen much of the time, and now we are starting to see this same pattern in the fire service and EMS.

Public Safety and Retirement

Retirement is supposed to be "the golden years" full of fun, travel, grandkids, and new endeavors. Why then, do so many public servants retire and crumble?

Retirement itself represents a huge transition. Many people in the midst of their careers look forward to one day retiring and being void of all the pressure, responsibilities, and obligations. When that time comes, however, it's not as easy as most people envision.

Retirement means change, and first responders detest change. Many first responders spend their entire careers complaining about change, even when it's change for the better. The changes that happen at retirement are monumental: in a moment, your purpose, passion, mission, schedule, structure, friends, and work family are all changed. They are busy at their regular work, which no longer includes you, and are for the most part gone.

First responders exist their entire lives at the top of the Maslow pyramid: self-actualization. Public safety professionals come to their careers with the desire to help others, heal pain, stop violence, prohibit death, and be there for others on the worst days of their lives. First responders spend their entire careers understanding they are a tiny piece of the puzzle of life who have something they can offer to others in an attempt to help them. This calling, this purpose, and this mission are a lifestyle and a part of each and every first responder. If they are not ready to shift their life in a big way at the end of their careers, first responders will not retire well.

What happens after retirement is something my practice has seen many times. If a first responder retires without proper planning, they will face a very uncomfortable adjustment period. The first thing public safety retirees notice is their schedule and routine have changed, which is very stressful on the brain and the body. We are creatures of habit, and suddenly everything gets thrown off by changes in eating and sleeping, for instance.

The next thing that happens is first responder retirees stop working out. Perhaps it's because they feel they no longer have to because they are no longer running calls; perhaps it's due to the changes in routine. Sometimes retirees stop working out because they miss their friends and their mission and are struggling with depression. Whatever the reason, the worst thing a retiree can do for their mental health is to quit working out. The biggest combatant for depression and the best stress management tool is exercise.

The loss of mission and purpose causes first responders to struggle as well. Suddenly they are no longer part of the fight. Their knowledge is considered outdated. Retirees who consider themselves inconsequential are forgetting about the many years when they were in the fight and on the front line, as well as the fact that it was an honor to hand their hard-gained experiences and this wild career off to the younger generation. The greatest skill of any craft is the ability to pass it down to the next group of young people to take the reins.

Then there is trauma. The brain has a funny way of managing trauma in retirees. Many first responders maintain a steady rate of being both busy and distracted during their careers. When retirement comes and first responders have slowed down and are not distracted by the tempo of emergency services, the brain has this unbelievable way of kicking off a mental shit storm of every bad call that happened in each person's career. The calls come back with a vengeance. Nightmares follow. Constant sights, smells, and sounds return to play in their minds. This feeling is absolutely miserable and most first responders attempt to stuff and ignore it. Without success.

I always tell first responder retirees this is normal. It's what you do NOW that counts. In retirement, with all of the distractions gone, the brain sometimes hands you what you have successfully suppressed for years. It's because you now have time and energy to deal with it. It is a very tough time for retirees, and many of them begin drinking heavily to cope. The decline that happens from trauma and copious alcohol as a coping mechanism is the beginning of the end. Retirees who do this will accelerate their demise. It is awful to watch.

When I was working in the emergency room, I had a small practice on the side. I worked weekends in the ER and weekdays in my office to build my practice. I lived in an area where a state trooper patrolled the nearby highways. He also lived in the same neighborhood. I would often see him running radar, see him in the ER, and in local businesses such as the grocery store. I got to know him by name, and we had the kind of relationship where we would always say "hi" to each other or he would flash his lights as we passed each other on the highway when I was going home in the morning and he was starting his shift.

This trooper was a formidable figure. He was 100 percent Texas State Trooper. He was tall—really tall with the hat on. His posture was always perfect, and he was clearly very strong based on his fitness. He emulated what most people envision when they envision a state trooper.

At some point, I stopped running into him. I assumed he had transferred somewhere else, or that we were just on different schedules. One day I walked into a coffee shop and I saw him. But what I saw I could not believe. It was as though someone had stuck a pin in this gentleman and he was deflating. He looked much older and smaller.

I approached him and he greeted me with a smile that was different, too. He looked weary. I asked him where he had been, and he explained to me that he retired six months ago. I asked him what he was doing now and his reply was "not much." At this point, I realized I had two choices. I could have wished him well and walked away or I could get in his business, which of course is what I did.

I asked this trooper if he was physically ill, and he told me he was not. I asked him how his life was and he responded, "It's fine." At this point I said exactly what was on my mind. "I see a man who is dying in front of me. I can tell you are struggling with retirement and my guess is that you are dealing with horrible demons from years of law enforcement work. I am begging you to come see me so I can help you. If not, you will continue to die, and I just can't stand it." My favorite trooper asked for my business card. He called and he came to every appointment. He is now happily retired, living his life to the fullest.

Retire the Right Way

The key to retiring the right way is planning, which starts two to three years out. Having a continued mission and purpose is essential to retiring right. Whether it is travel, a second (or third) career, hobbies, volunteering, raising grandkids, or a combination of many things, it is important to stay engaged. Having plans with purpose and meaning, staying on a routine or schedule, and continuing to exercise is imperative for both mental and physical health.

The other component of planning is to conquer the demons before you leave your career. Take time in your final year to sit with a clinician and work through those tough calls that just won't let you go. Resolve the traumas and spend time working on your resilience. Leave with a clean slate and plans that make you wonder how you ever had time to have a job.

I worked with a police chief who came to the practice about a year before he retired. He told me that he fully intended to continue to live and that he wanted to learn how to be a civilian. As he worked though his demons from his early patrol days, he remarked at how much he had suppressed some really bad traumas, including witnessing a line-of-duty death of a fellow officer. To get it resolved was hard work but successful work. He was serious about becoming "a civilian." He started to grow his hair out during his last year. I jokingly referred to him as "my hippie patient."

Special Considerations for Loved Ones

As first responders retire, family members will also face an adjustment period. It is remarkable how family members adjust to the tempo and schedules of public service, and how they then have to re-adjust when getting away from it, as well. As a career comes to an end, it will be different at home. The most significant thing I hear from family members is having to get used to how much time you now have together. Ease into this, enjoy it, and make the most of it. Your brains and bodies will adapt, too.

Chapter Nine

This is Our War

Tongue tied, dead inside
Nothing left, not even pride
This isn't how I thought the future would go
Hell-bent, soul is spent
Nothing left but to repent
I've gotta dig myself right out of this hole
This isn't my fight
This is my war

"This Is My War" by Five Finger Death Punch

First responders are valuable assets. They are trained, skilled, and dedicated individuals who commit their lives and careers to helping others. We ask our first responders to enter danger, trauma, tragedy—the worst situations—and take control of them. We ask them to come to work during disasters when the rest of the city is hunkering down or evacuating. Yet somehow, the system frequently fails to care for first responders, either adequately or not at all.

I am challenging public safety professionals and leadership to take this on and begin to change the culture. By changing the culture, we change the narrative. The narrative must be that no one is immune to stress and trauma, and by making sure needed resources are in place, we can assure that first responders will not just survive—they will thrive—in their careers.

On the Line

I ask first responders to change the culture and the narrative by really looking out for each other. Getting educated on normal reactions to stress, how to manage stress, and when to know that further help is needed is an important survival tool in emergency services. Looking out for your colleagues keeps everyone safer and more resilient.

The days of "suck it up" are over. I always say that "suck it up" is what we do to get through the fight or to get that patient to the ER. In the aftermath, however, if we continue to "suck it up," it usually leads to "drink it off" and other bad habits.

I also ask first responders to remember that events impact us in different ways. When our resilience is low or we are going through tough times, a non-problematic call to you might be a tough one for your partner. Please don't look at your partner and ask, "What the hell is wrong with you?" Instead please ask, "Hey, are you okay?"

You all owe it to each other to look out for each other. If a crazed individual high on methamphetamines laced with PCP is charging at your partner with a butcher knife, you will be there 100 percent to help them. During tough times when a partner seems stressed or distant, many first responders don't know what to do or say, so they turn away. Instead, I ask first responders to check in with each other, to let your partner know that you are there, and to ask if there is a way you can help them.

This is a culture change. It will not sissify public safety. The point is to tackle demons, improve resilience, and stay healthy.

Leadership

The first and most important step is to assure that a good plan is in place. In *First Responder Resilience: Caring for Public Servants,* I outline the elements of a good plan. Setting things in motion through peer support training and recruiting qualified mental health professionals to help out is a great start. Refining your plan as you go and making it fit your department's needs is imperative. Having policies to back up your mental health plan is also a must.

Make the focus all about prevention and resilience. Don't approach a traumatic event with a "wait and see" mindset. Instead, begin caring for hearts and minds immediately. Set the tone that it is okay to ask for help and encourage it.

As with any good program, there is cost. Leaders

sometimes get caught up in adding a budget item and the impact on the rest of the budget, yet somehow there is always enough money budgeted for replacing first responders who quit. The turnover rates in public safety are remarkably high. The average cost to put a police officer through the academy is $60,000. Considering that based on the cost of training and establishing a working Peer Support Team, and the possibility that your Peer Support Team helps just one employee through tough times or burnout and prevents them from quitting, will prove that your Peer Support Team has more than paid for itself.

Check your attitude about getting help. As a leader, your first responders are more likely to ask for help when you get help yourself and promote it. When you don't get help yourself, neither will your people. Please don't adopt a "do as I say, not as I do" attitude about asking for help.

I worked with a police officer who was hit by a car while he was on the side of a highway. He sustained multiple injuries but was able to return to work. His chief was concerned because he started receiving complaints about the officer yelling at the public, being overly aggressive and extremely hostile. This officer was struggling with PTSD. This officer denied all of it. He denied having any problems and even denied having any sort of reaction to the incident. He attempted to portray himself as totally immune and refused all help. On his way out the door, he told me that he had accepted a job as the chief of police of a neighboring town. He also told me that he does not believe in PTSD and that he would not be setting up any mental health programs due to his knowledge that it does not exist. In this day and age, considering all of the knowledge we have gained regarding PTSD ever since the war in Vietnam, such an attitude is the worst possible any leader can have. It is inexcusable.

Finally, please consider this: first responders are not disposable. First responders who struggle are frequently seen as burdens or as problems. Instead of asking what has happened to someone who is struggling, those around that person will simply remark how they have changed or how bad their attitude is. Leaders who do not take the time to understand what is going on with someone who is struggling will simply try to push them out.

First responders DO recover from burnout, trauma, and PTSD. They return to the line with wisdom and resilience. They make some of the best employees you will ever have the privilege of leading, because they understand themselves and others. After recovering from trauma, first responders have more compassion, patience, and insight. They become experts in handling the public and in looking out for their fellow first responders. We call this post-traumatic growth. The magic words I hear in my office every day as people achieve post-traumatic growth: "I wouldn't wish this on anyone, but this experience has made me better, stronger, and

Code Four: Surviving and Thriving in Public Safety

wiser." We should all be so lucky to have first responders on our team who have reached post-traumatic growth.

Three Air Evac personnel who achieved post-traumatic growth and are paying it forward by going through peer support training

Resource List for First Responders

Institute for Responder Wellness: 877.225.5443

Blue H.E.L.P: weabluehelp.org

National Suicide Prevention Lifeline: 1.800.273.8255

Veterans Crisis Line: 1.800.273.8255

Copline (Law Enforcement): 1.800.267.5463

Crisis Text Line: Crisistextline.org or text 741741

HOPE Animal Assisted Crisis Response: Hopeaacr.org

Tania Glenn: www.taniaglenn.com

About the Author

Tania was three months from completing her Master's Degree at the University of Texas when she witnessed the dramatic and violent standoff between law enforcement and the Branch Davidian Cult in Waco, Texas. At that point, she knew her calling was to work with first responders and to focus on healing these warriors from the horrors of post-traumatic stress disorder.

Tania spent the first ten years of her career working in a Level Two Trauma Emergency Department on weekend nights as she built her private practice during the week. In 2002, Tania transitioned to her private practice on a full-time basis and has dedicated her entire career to working with first responders and military members.

Tania assisted with the aftermath of the Oklahoma City Murrah Federal Building bombing, the 9/11 attacks on the World Trade Center, Hurricane Katrina, the Dallas Police shootings, and numerous other incidents. Tania is referred to as the "warrior healer" by her colleagues, and she is passionate about her work.

Tania resides in Central Texas. Her loves include her family, her pets and fitness.

Tania has two other books published by Progressive Rising Phoenix Press:
First Responder Resilience: Caring for Public Servants Protected But Scared